Ancient Testaments of the
Patriarchs

Autobiographies from the Dead Sea Scrolls

By Ken Johnson, Th.D.

Copyright 2017, by Ken Johnson, Th.D.

Ancient Testaments of the Patriarchs
by Ken Johnson, Th.D.

Printed in the United States of America

ISBN – 10: 978-1975887742
ISBN – 13: 1975887743

Unless otherwise indicated, Bible quotations are taken from the King James Version.

Contents

Introduction 4
Enoch's Prophecies 8
The Testaments 10
    Testament of Enos 11
    Testament of Lamech 14
    Testament of Noah 22
    Testament of Abraham 32
    Testament of Jacob 42
    Testament of Reuben 45
    Testament of Simeon 51
    Testament of Levi 56
    Testament of Judah 71
    Testament of Issachar 86
    Testament of Zebulun 91
    Testament of Dan 98
    Testament of Naphtali 103
    Testament of Gad 112
    Testament of Asher 117
    Testament of Joseph 123
    Testament of Benjamin 136
    Testament of Kohath 144
    Testament of Amram 147
    Testament of Aaron 152
Prophecy Outline 155
The Jubilee Prophecy 159
Related Dead Sea Scrolls 164
Other Books by Ken Johnson, Th.D. 168
Bibliography 170

Ancient Testaments of the Patriarchs

Introduction

The history of the Dead Sea Scrolls is very complex. We know that the Essenes kept an ancient library in Qumran. We also know that sometime before the Roman destruction of the Jerusalem Temple in AD 70, the Essenes sealed the scrolls of their library in jars for a future generation. Through the ages there were times when Bedouins sought to sell scrolls they found in caves near, or around, Jerusalem.

One such report was by the Syrian Patriarch in the eleventh century. He offered to buy any scrolls that were ancient copies of the books of the Bible. By the late 1700's, many such rumors abounded. One set of scrolls came to light. They were called the *Testaments of the Twelve Patriarchs*. These were supposedly the writings of the twelve sons of Jacob: Ruben, Simeon, Levi, Judah, Issachar, Zebulun, Dan, Naphtali, Gad, Asher, Joseph, and Benjamin. They were their last words to their children dealing mainly with morality; but also containing references to ancient prophecy.

Scholars had two major problems with these testaments. First, the prophecies were very focused on the Messiah and agreed wholeheartedly with Christian doctrine. Second, the story was that the original Hebrew version was in the hands of a private collector and only the retranslated Greek was available for scholars to study.

Introduction

With no original Hebrew scrolls and messianic prophecies being too Christian-like, the *Testaments of the Twelve Patriarchs* were dubbed to be Christian fiction. They are still part of volume eight of the *Ante-Nicene Fathers* (ten volume set) that was produced in the late 1800's. All that changed with the official discovery of the Dead Sea Scrolls.

Between AD 1948 to 2016, twelve caves were found in Qumran containing many ancient scrolls that are pre-Christian. A forty-volume set of the Dead Sea Scrolls was produced entitled *Discoveries in the Judean Desert*. This set contains every photo, description, and translation of these scrolls. Fragments of five of the twelve sons of Jacob were found in the Dead Sea Scrolls: Levi, Judah, Naphtali, Joseph, and Benjamin. In this book, the portions of the twelve that were found in the Dead Sea Scrolls are underlined, so that you can see how much remains from the original Hebrew.

The Other Testaments

The legend found in the Talmud of the orthodox Jews and in the Essene community is that all of the patriarchs from Adam to Aaron (thirty-seven or more) were prophets and all wrote testaments for their posterity. Aaron started a new temporary priesthood that would exist until the time of what Elijah called the Messianic Age. We call this the church age. What is truly amazing is that not only do the Dead Sea Scrolls tell us of this legend, and contain five of the twelve testaments of the sons of Jacob, but they

Ancient Testaments of the Patriarchs actually contain fragments of eight of the other testaments as well.

We have fragments of the testaments of: Enos (Adam's Grandson), Enoch, Lamech (Noah's Father), Noah, Abraham, Jacob, Levi, Judah, Naphtali, Joseph, Benjamin, Kohath (son of Levi, and father of Amram), Amram (father of Moses, Aaron, and Miriam), and Aaron.

The information given in these Dead Sea Scroll fragments is identical to the information given in the full Latin versions of the *Testaments of the Twelve Patriarchs* published in the late 1800's.

We have a modern English version of the *Ancient Book of Enoch* translated from the Ethiopic version (full book) compared to the fragments of Enoch found in the Dead Sea Scrolls.

When looking at a Dead Sea Scroll, it will have a title like 1Q21. The *Testament of Levi* is 1Q21. The "Q" in this designation means it was found in Qumran. The number "1" means it was found in cave one of the twelve caves. The "21" means it was the twenty-first scroll found in that cave.

The book of Jubilees mentions the herbal medicine books of Noah and Shem (10:13), the books of Noah's fathers (12:27), the books of Enoch, Noah, and the forefathers (21:10), and the book of Amram (46:10). Jubilees 45:16 states that Jacob gave all of these books of the fathers to

Introduction

Levi. Jubilees 32:21-26 states that Jacob was buried with a copy of his testament. Maybe that and other testaments are buried with the patriarchs in the cave of Machpelah in Hebron.

Dead Sea Scroll Testaments

Enosh (4Q369)	Judah (3Q7, 4Q538-9)
Enoch (4Q201)	Naphtali (4Q215)
Lamech (1Q20, 4Q535)	Benjamin (1Q538)
Noah (1Q19, 1Q20)	Kohath (4Q542)
Abraham (1Q20)	Amram (4Q543-549)
Jacob (4Q537)	Aaron (4Q540, 4Q541)
Levi (1Q21)	

Enoch's Prophecies

Most the prophecies given in these testaments are based, as they state, on older testaments we do not have. We do have the book of Enoch, which is often quoted in these testaments as authoritative. Before we begin our study of these testaments, we should take a moment to look at some of the prophecies given by Enoch. Here are the charts given on pages 10-12 of the *Ancient Book of Enoch*.

Biblical Doctrines Found in Enoch	Enoch	Bible
No flesh is righteous before the Lord	81:5	Rom. 3:10
Abortion is murder	98:5; 99:5	Ex. 21:22-23
God is omniscient and omnipotent	9:5	Jer. 23:24
Flood covered the entire earth	106:15	Gen. 7:19
Noah and family spent one year in the ark	106:15	Gen. 7:11; 8:14
Meditation (sorcery) blinds men to God	99:8	Rom. 1:21
Denying inspiration is calling God a liar	104:9	2 Tim. 3:16
All pre-flood men and giants perished	89:6	Gen. 7:4
Do not alter the Scripture	104:9	Rev. 22:18-19
Ignoring prophecy is a serious sin	108:6	Luk. 24:25
Book of Enoch not to be added to the Bible	104	Rev. 22:18

Doctrines About the Messiah	Enoch	Bible
Messiah is the Son of God	105:2	1 Jn. 5:5
Salvation hangs on the Messiah	40:5	Acts 4:12
Salvation by repentance and belief in His Name	50:2-3	Luk. 13:3
Salvation by believing on the Messiah's name	45:3; 48:7	Acts 4:12
Salvation by the righteousness of faith	39:6	Rom. 4:11
Messiah's name (Yeshua) is hinted at	5:7	Isa. 12:2-3
Messiah is called the "Word"	90:38	Joh. 1:1
Messiah is called the Son of Man	48:10	Mat. 9:6
Son of Man exists with God the Father eternally	48:6	2 Sam. 7:14
Messiah's shed blood is necessary for salvation	47:2,4	Mat. 26:28
Son of Man existed before any created thing	48:2-3, 6	Ps. 102:25-27
Messiah preserves the righteous	48:7	Jn. 17:12
Messiah will be a light unto the nations	48:4	Isa. 42:6

Enoch's Prophecies

First Coming Prophecies	Enoch	Bible
Messiah born of a virgin	62:5	Isa. 7:14
Jews will deny the Messiah	48:10	Joh. 1:11
Elect One will resurrect from the dead	51:5	Joh. 21:14
Bible given to the righteous	104	2 Tim. 3:16
The Righteous One will resurrect	92:3	Joh. 21:14
The Righteous One will give eternal life	5:9; 92:4	Joh. 10:28
Man errs respecting time and the calendar	75:2, 82:5,9	Luk. 19:44

End Time Prophecies	Enoch	Bible
Angels will never crossbreed again	68:5	-
Corrupted Bibles will be created	99,104	Rev. 22:18-19
Jude's quote of Enoch	1:9	Jud. 1:14-15
Everyone will kneel before the Messiah	48:5; 57:3	Phil. 2:10
The Rapture (taking out of the midst) occurs	70:2	2 Thess. 2:7
Everyone will resurrect	62:5	Rev. 20:5
"Valley of dry bones" mentioned	90:4	Ezek. 37:4
Years will be shortened	80:2	Mat. 24:22
The Rapture and Resurrection are a mystery	103:2	1 Cor. 15:51
Rapture before the Tribulation to cause repentance	50:1-5	Dan. 12:3
Rapture mentioned as "the Mercy"	1:8; 5:5	Jud. 1:21
Truth altered in the latter days	104:10-13	Rev. 22:18-19
Iran will attack Israel, God sends confusion	56:5-7	Ezek. 38-39
Days will be shortened	80:2	Mat. 24:22
The moon will change its order	80:4	Rev. 6:12-13
There will be blood up to a horse's breast	100:3	Rev. 14:20
Millennium mortals and immortals dwell together	39:1	Rev. 20:4
There will be 7000 years of history	93	-

If we understand that the writers of the testaments reproduced in this volume were very familiar with these prophecies given by Enoch, we can better understand their writings.

Ancient Testaments of the Patriarchs

The Testaments

Testament of Enos

4Q369

Fragment 1 Col 1

...all the mysteries. The angel of your peace will... until the guilty repent... all of the festivals in their periods because from old You have engraved Your marvelous...

...His judgement until the ordained time of judgement as recorded in the eternal commands. [My son,] Cainan was the fourth generation; Mahalalel, his son, was the fifth generation; Jared, his son, was the sixth generation; Enoch, his son, was the seventh generation...

Fragment 1 Col 2

You have divided Your name for his inheritance, so that he may establish Your name there. She [the holy city] is the glory of Your earthly kingdom. You will eternally watch over her and Your glory will manifest there. She will be an eternal passion throughout all generations to His seed. By Your righteous judgment, You will purify Him to be an eternal light. You have made Him a firstborn son to You. He will be a prince and ruler of Your earthly kingdom. You have placed the crown of the heavens and the glory of the clouds upon Him. You have placed the angel of Your peace in His congregation and given Him laws of righteousness as a father does for his son. He loves You and He has your Spirit. Through them You establish Your glory.

Ancient Testaments of the Patriarchs

Fragment 2
...and prison. Angels intercede and to fight against all lands... You judge and recompense them for their works...

Fragment 3
You rule all that is, and You give honor to whom You will. You hold all the dominions in Your hand, and call each one by name...

Fragment 4
times of dominion... in the generations...appointed times...

Fragment 5
Without you...

Commentary
Fragment 1, Column 1 has been classified as part of the *Testament of Enos*, partly because he begins a chronology with his son Cainan. God is sovereign and He has made unchangeable decrees that include true law, repentance (Teshuva), festivals for signs, and a future time of judgment.

Fragment 1, Column 2, seems to teach that the capital pre-flood city would be rebuilt afterwards and be the center

Testament of Enos

for God's glory again. It was first called Salem, but then was later renamed Jerusalem. It then describes either Abraham, who fathered the nation of Israel, or the Messiah, who came from that nation to bring salvation to all mankind.

Fragment 2 seems to be stating there are angels of countries that fight for control. God judges each situation, punishing some and forgiving others.

Fragments 3-5 are too small to really understand the complete context. They seem to indicate that God is in control and has decreed certain ages where certain powers rule, but ultimately God is always in control and evil will be judged in the Day of Judgment. There is also a mention of the Moedim, the appointed times.

Testament of Lamech

1Q20, cols. 0-5

The Testament of Lamech is found in 1Q20 which is commonly call the *Genesis Apocryphon*. It is fragmented but reproduced here. Enoch tells this same story in his testament, which is found in chapter 106-107 of the Ethiopic book of Enoch, also reproduced here. The Dead Sea Scroll is as follows:

Column 0

…and all of us from… so in each way we may consent in this adulterous act… all that you will… you will amplify anger and it will be unstoppable, for who is there…who… in the heat of anger… the simple, the humble, and the lowly shake and tremble… We are now imprisoned! …to cease from your anger… by your anger…since we will leave the house of…the Great Holy One… Now your hand is ready to strike …and to destroy all… because he ceased speaking when we were imprisoned… a fire that has appeared… before the Lord of Heaven… and attacking them from behind. And no longer… seek grace and mercy from the Lord of Eternity…before the Lord of Eternity.

Testament of Lamech

Column 1

...descended, and with the women... and the mystery of iniquity[a] that... times, and the mystery that... we did not reveal... not... until the day... the mystery, whether they are all your sons, or... great... witchcraft, sorcery, and divinations... the earth, and I will begin... part of the deed up till now...which is upon dry ground, to establish... see, I have given all of them... and if... those who strike against... their strong bond... from... all flesh is cursed... the Lord, who sent messengers to you... to the earth, and to descend to strengthen the people ...teach what to do. Men of earth... he did not to them only but all flesh...

Column 2

It suddenly occurred to me that the conception could be from Watchers, or the seed from Holy Ones, or Nephilim. My mind wavered concerning the baby. Then I, Lamech, was so upset, I came to Batenosh[b], my wife, and said to her... I swear by the Most High, the Mighty Lord, the King of all Ages... one of the sons of Heaven. So, you must tell the whole truth to me, no matter... you have to [truthfully] recount for me, no lies! Will you give birth to a son that is unique? Then Batenosh, my wife, started crying and pleading with me... she said, "My brother, my husband, you have to remember the time of our love, my pleasure... the heat of the moment, and my panting

---

[a] 2 Thessalonians 2:7
[b] Bath-Enos or daughter of Enos. This is the same name given to her in the Book of Jubilees.

breath! I swear I have told you everything truthfully..." But I did not believe her. When Batenosh, my wife, saw that my demeanor had changed to anger, she calmed down and said to me, "My husband, my brother, my pleasure, I swear to you by the Great Holy One, the King of Heaven, that this baby is yours, yours! You are the father! I have not slept with any stranger, Watcher, nor son of Heaven. Why do I see sadness in your eyes and your doubt on your face, when I tell you the truth?" Then I, Lamech, ran to Methuselah my father and told him and asked him to ask his father Enoch what the dream actually means because he know the Watchers well and God makes everything known to him. Methuselah, my father, understood the importance of the dream and went to Enoch, his father, in the land of Parvain, which is called the "ends of the earth," to find out the truth. He said to Enoch, his father, "My father and my lord, I have come to you... do not to be angry that I came here to seek you..."

Column 3

For in the days of Jared my father... where the sons of Heaven dwelt... human houses... and upon... over all the earth... from my land to that sea... he will place all of it as one fruit. ...he called his people. Now go... truthfully, without lies... reaches by way of a spring to... he is the one who will divide the entire earth, and with... he made sure Methuselah, his son, understood... to him that in every sea... the Lord will give him an everlasting name... from her womb...

Testament of Lamech

Column 4
Now... they will be the cause of much evil... for all ages... I passed judgment upon ... the name of the Great Holy One, and an end... them from the face of the earth...

Column 5
He wrote all of them in the scroll as a remembrance, all... "Methuselah, my son, this child... for when I, Enoch... not from the sons of Heaven, but from Lamech your son... he resembles... because of his appearance your son Lamech was afraid... Go, tell Lamech, your son, that the child is truly his, not from the sons of Heaven... He will be exalted on the earth, and be a judge over every man... that he lifted his face and his eyes shone like the sun, this means that...not the seed of a stranger... They will be caught and destroyed by their own impurity... they will act with much violence until they boil over, and every path of violence... make sure your son knows this mystery... what will occur in his days... blessing the Lord of All... When Methuselah understood the interpretation, and revealed it to Lamech, his son, the mystery... When I, Lamech, understood... rejoiced in the Lord...

Enoch's Account of Lamech's Dream
In the *Ancient Book of Enoch* 106-107, Enoch describes the same events.

Enoch 106 - Lamech's Dream
After some time, my son Methuselah took a wife for his son Lamech, and she became pregnant by him and bore a

son. ²His body was white as snow and red as the blooming of a rose, and the hair of his head was white as wool, and his eyes were beautiful. When he opened his eyes, they lit up the whole house like the sun, and the whole house was very bright. ³When he was taken from the hands of the midwife, he opened his mouth, and spoke to the Lord of Righteousness. ⁴His father Lamech was afraid of him, and fled, and came to his father Methuselah. ⁵He said unto him: "I have begotten a strange son, unlike a man, but resembling the sons of the angels of heaven; and his nature is different. He is not like us; and his eyes are as the rays of the sun, and his countenance is beautiful. ⁶It seems to me that he is not sprung from me but from the angels, and I fear that awful things will happen on the earth in his days."

Lamech Seeks Enoch's Interpretation
⁷"Now, my father, I am here to ask and implore you to go to our father, Enoch, and learn the truth from him, for his dwelling place is with the angels."

⁸When Methuselah heard the words of his son, he came to me at the ends of the earth, for he had heard that I was there, and he cried aloud. I heard his voice and I came to him. I said unto him, "Behold, here am I, my son. Why have you come to me?"

⁹He answered and said, "I have come to you because of a disturbing vision which has caused me great anxiety, ¹⁰and now, my father, hear me. Unto Lamech, my son, there was born a son, whose likeness and nature were

unlike other men. His color was whiter than snow and redder than the bloom of a rose, and the hair of his head was whiter than white wool, and his eyes were like the rays of the sun, and when he opened his eyes he illuminated the whole house. ¹¹When he arose in the hands of the midwife, he opened his mouth, and spoke to the Lord of heaven. ¹²His father Lamech was afraid and fled to me, and did not believe that the child sprang from him, because his likeness was like that of the angels of heaven. Behold, I have come to you that you may tell me the truth."

Enoch Interprets the Dream

¹³I, Enoch, answered and said unto him, "The Lord will do a new thing on the earth, and this I have already seen in a vision. I need to tell you that in the generation of my father Jared, some of the angels of heaven transgressed the word of the Lord. ¹⁴They committed sin and transgressed the law by uniting themselves with women. They committed sin with them, and have married some of them, and have begotten children by them. ¹⁵A great destruction will come over the whole earth, and there will be a flood of water and a great destruction for one year.[c] ¹⁶This son who was born unto you will be left on the earth; and his three children will be saved with him. When all mankind who are left on the earth will die, he and his sons will be saved. ¹⁷They who begot giants on the earth, not according to the Spirit, but according to the

---

[c] Genesis 7:11 and 8:14

flesh, will suffer a great punishment on the earth, and the earth will be cleansed from all impurity.

18 Now make known to your son Lamech that he who will be born is truly his son. Call his name Noah, for he will be left to you; and he and his sons will be saved from the destruction which will come upon the earth on account of all the sin and all the unrighteousness which will be consummated on the earth in his days. 19 After that, there will be still more unrighteousness than that which was first committed on the earth; for I know the mysteries of the holy ones; for He, the Lord, has showed me and informed me, and I have read them in the heavenly tablets.

Enoch 107 - The Flood Will Not Be the Complete End

I saw written on them that generation upon generation will transgress, till a generation of righteousness arises, and transgression is destroyed and sin disappears from the earth, and all manner of good comes upon it. ²Now, my son, go and tell your son Lamech that this son, which will be born, really will be his son, and that this is no lie." ³When Methuselah had heard the words of his father Enoch — for he had shown to him everything in secret — he returned with the interpretation and explained it to him and called the name of that son Noah; for he will comfort[d] the earth after all the destruction.

---

[d] Noah means "rest" or "comfort" in Hebrew.

Testament of Lamech

Commentary

Columns 0-1 are a retelling of the descent of the Watchers, their sin with the women of earth, and the race of Nephilim. The angels were to teach mankind to be godly; but they corrupted mankind instead, by teaching witchcraft, sorcery, divination, and other dark arts. God then judged the angels and sent the Flood of Noah to cleanse the earth for a new beginning.

In Column 2, Lamech has a fight with his wife about the dream he had concerning her pregnancy. He asked his father Methuselah to ask his grandfather Enoch to interpret the dream.

Columns 3-5 are Enoch's explanation to Methuselah about Noah. Enoch's account of this from his book, chapters 106-107, are also given here for reference.

Ancient Testaments of the Patriarchs

Testament of Noah

1Q20, cols. 6-18

The *Testament of Noah* actually starts on the last line of Col 5 which says:

"A copy of the book of the words of Noah..."

The rest of the testament is continued in Columns 6 through 18.

Column 6

From my birth my mother taught me in the ways of righteousness. My whole life I walked in the truth of the Holy One as He had instructed. I kept away from the paths of deceit which lead to eternal darkness. I studied the visions of truth and wisdom, praying ceaselessly, and avoided the paths of violence. Even after becoming an adult, I continued in righteousness, grew in wisdom... I married Emzera,[e] his daughter, and she bore me three sons... and daughters. Later I took three of the daughters of my brothers for wives for my sons, according to the marriage custom that the Lord of Eternity gave to Adam. After many years, about ten jubilees, after the time when

---

[e] Emzera can be translated as "seed of my people." In other words, he married a godly relative. According to the *Ancient Book of Jasher*, Noah married Namaah, daughter of Enoch

my sons should have been married, the Lord appeared to me in a vision. He showed me the conduct of the sons of Heaven. I thought about this mystery a lot but did not tell anyone about the vision... the great Holy One sent the Watcher to instruct me. In the vision, he said, in a loud voice, "they are talking about you, Noah" ... I considered their behavior and knew who would succeed. After two weeks... bore witness to all the blood shed by the Nephilim... I waited until... the daughters of men whom the holy ones made unclean by divination. I went and asked one of them... I, Noah, found grace, prominence, and righteousness in the eyes of the Lord... to cattle, wild animals, birds and even humans... the entire deed was very...

Column 7

"You will govern the entire earth; all that is upon it, including the mountains and the seas... forbid the worship of all the host of heaven; the sun, moon, stars, and the Watchers. ...the great Holy One." Then I rejoiced at the words of the Lord of Heaven... He will make them pure by the blood upon... through you all humanity... this was my dream. So, I blessed the great Holy One, and gave thanks for the knowledge of what is to come. I made this known only to my family...

Column 8

...throughout the entire flood ... the King of Heaven... in your week... everything occurring in its week. In the written account, its week... about three weeks... Then I went...

Column 9

... your father... not spare... My decrees are irrevocable...

Column 10[f]

Then I blessed the Lord of All, who kept me safe... I, Noah, spoke of these words to them... Now go, give praise and glory to the Creator... remember the instructions of our Lord, who is the King of all Ages forever and ever.

The ark rested on one of the mountains of Ararat, and the eternal fire... I atoned for the whole earth. First, I offered a male goat... afterward I burned the fat upon the fire. Second, I offered a thank offering consisting of ox, ram, and sheep. Then I poured out all of their blood on the base of the altar and, and burned all of their flesh on the altar. Third, I offered the young turtledoves (flesh and blood) with them upon the altar. Then I offered fine wheat flour, mixed together with oil containing incense, for their meal offerings. I said a blessing, and was putting salt on all of them, and the scent of my offering rose up to the heavens. Then the Most High blessed...

Column 11

I, Noah, was at the door of the ark when the waters receded... my sons and their sons... the mountains, valleys, wildernesses, and the coastlands, all... Then I,

---

[f] Compare to Jubilees 21.

Testament of Noah

Noah, went out and walked through the breadth and depth of the land... it had been reborn with grass, herbs, grain, and fruit trees with leaves. Then I blessed the Lord of Heaven, glory to Him! He showed His love for His creation by removing and obliterating all those who practiced violence, wickedness, and deceit, but rescued the righteous man... A heavenly one appeared to me and said, "Do not fear, Noah! I will be with you and all of your sons who will be like you, forever. Be fruitful and multiply, and fill the earth. Rule over all of them; over its seas and over its wildernesses, over its mountains and over everything that is in them. I now give everything to you and your sons for food; that of the vegetation and herbs of the land. But all blood you will not eat..."

Column 12

"I have now placed My bow in the clouds, and it is a sign from Me, in order to be... on the mountains of Ararat." After this, I left the mountain. My sons and I had to rebuild the cities, because the devastation was great. Then my sons had many sons and daughters after the flood. My oldest son Shem had a son, Arpachshad, two years after the flood. All the sons of Shem, were: Elam, Asshur, Arpachshad, Lud, and Aram, with five daughters. The sons of Ham were: Cush, Mitzraim, Put, and Canaan, with seven daughters. The sons of Japheth were: Gomer, Magog, Madai, Javan, Tubal, Meshech, and Tiras, with four daughters. My sons and I began to plant crops. I planted a great vineyard on Mount Lubar, and in four years it produced great amounts of wine for me. I brought out all the wine when the first feast came.ᵍ On the first day of the first feast, in the first month… in the midst of my vineyard, I opened this vessel, and began to drink from it on the first day of the fifth year of the vineyard. On that day, I, my sons and grandsons, with all of our wives and daughters, gathered together at the altar. I blessed the Lord of Heaven, the Most High God, the great Holy One, who saved us from the destruction… which my fathers hid and… I laid down upon my bed, and my mind stirred…

Column 13 – the Dream
"…to you, Noah, the king, …and the decree… to all the forests with all the birds of heaven, the beasts of the field, the cattle of the land, and the creeping things of the dry ground… The stones and the clay were cutting down the forest to make it a place for themselves. Then, also, the gold, silver, brass, and iron, were cutting down the forest to make it a place for themselves. Then I watched as the sun, moon, and stars cut down part of the forest to make it theirs. Finally, the swarming things of the earth and water consumed it. When the water ceased, it ended… Then I saw that the olive tree had grown tall! It continued to grow for many hours, with beautiful fruit, a great amount of foliage. I wondered about this olive tree, with its abundance of leaves… everything tying ropes onto it. Then the winds of heaven blew violently against this olive

---

ᵍ Jewish tradition says this was Rosh Hashanah, the Jewish New Year.

tree, ripping off its branches and breaking it to pieces. First, a wind blew in from... west. It struck it, causing its leaves and fruit to fall from it, and scattered it to the winds. After this... and a northern wind from..."

Column 14

"...you were thinking about the tree with its upper branch separating and budding with much fruit and foliage... Understand that you are the great cedar tree that was standing before you on a mountain top in your dream. The shoots which emerged from it and grew equal to its height are your three sons... The first shoot that you saw adhering to the cedar trunk, with one branch separating from it and becoming an olive tree means the first son will not separate from you for all his days, and among his seed your name will be called.[h] From his division, all your sons [will be blessed] and from him, the first son, will come forth as a righteous planting [the nation of Israel] for all... standing fast forever. The second shoot adhering to the trunk of the cedar tree... The branch of the third shoot... brings the darkness, and a few of their boughs that enter into the midst of the boughs of the first one, represent two sons [Canaan and Nimrod] ... one south and one north of the land. As for their few boughs that enter into the midst of the boughs of the first one, the descendants of this shoot will invade his land by the coastlands of the Great Sea, and not... to understand the mystery, after your death... you will search... The

---

[h] Compare to Genesis 21:12 and Hebrews 11:18.

mystery of... entering into it, and the first one... for himself above all their gods which... for himself... in an allotment in Amania, next to Elam [Iran]... the Great Sea [Mediterranean Sea] ... serve, first, exchanging his allotment for an allotment."

Column 15

"...of the Merciful One on all of those who multiply wickedness in your land and to the ends of the earth. You saw all of those crying out and turning away, because most them will be evil. The great warrior coming from the southern part of the land, with the sickle in His hand and the fire with Him, He will crush all... This one is the Mighty Lord who will come from the southern part of the land... the torches and the evil one. Then He will throw all the rebellious ones into the fire and seal the pit. As to those who were plucked up...south."

"...four mighty angels chained away from all the peoples of the earth who will not have power over the agitated one [Antichrist] because of their conduct, their inadvertent error, and their undecidedness because of the great blasphemer [False Prophet] ... He [Messiah] will couple this people to Himself. He will cut out a great mountain; and from it He will consecrate and separate between all the nations, those who serve Him and those who are entangled with... You, Noah, do not be amazed at this dream, and may no evil be added to it... I have revealed everything to you truthfully, as it is written concerning you. Some of your people will join you..." Then I, Noah, awoke. It was morning and I blessed the everlasting God.

Testament of Noah

I quickly went to Shem, my son, and told him everything, that through him the Righteous One would come, and that he had to preserve the knowledge and become the next priest of the Most High God."

Column 16 - Land of Shem and Japheth ~ Jubilees 8
...river, west until it reaches the sea that is between them; the source of the Ma'uk up to the Tina River. It runs through the entire length of the land of the north until it reaches its source in the Rafa mountain range. The boundary extends to the waters of the Great Sea until it reaches Gadir... This is the division that Noah gave to Japheth and his children as an eternal inheritance. Shem inherited the second portion, for himself and his children forever... where Tina River emerges, toward... the Me'at Sea, which reaches... the gulf of the Great Salt Sea. This boundary goes from the spring to the gulf... the gulf of the sea that faces Egypt.... Ham inherited the southern portion for himself and his children forever... Gihon River toward the south...

Column 17 – Divisions of Shem's and Japheth's Sons
Shem divided his portion between his sons. Elam inherited the area in the north, along the Tigris River, until it reaches the Erythrean Sea, to its source which is in the north. Asshur inherited the area toward the west, until it reaches the Tigris... Aram inherited the land between the two rivers until it reaches the peak of Mount Ararat, at this settlement. Lud... inherited the Mount Taurus. This portion continues west until it reaches Magog; everything along the... eastern gulf, in the north, touching this gulf...

which is above the three portions in the south. Arpachshad… turns to the south; the entire land irrigated by the Euphrates, and all… the valleys and the plains that are between them, and the coastlands… Amana, which extends from Mount Ararat to the Euphrates… These are Shem's divisions. Japheth divided his portion between his sons. Gomer inherited the northern region that touches Tina River. After him lies the land of Magog, then the land of Madai, then the land of Javan, including all the islands and the gulf alongside Lud. Tubal inherited the land across the second gulf. Meshech inherited… Tiras inherited four islands, within the Great Sea that touches Ham's portion… These are the portions of Japheth that Noah gave him for allotments for his sons.

Column 18
This column was left blank.

Commentary
Columns 6-7 give an account of Noah's life and the visions he had about the fallen angels, the Nephilim, the genetic tampering, and the coming flood. After the flood, he is to rule all nations and forbid any form of idolatry. The middle of Column 7 reveals a descendant of Noah would cleanse all mankind though His blood.

Columns 8-9 are badly fragmented but seem to show Noah aboard the ark, waiting for the waters to recede, spending his time looking over the written prophecies handed down by his fathers. He mentions a prophecy of weeks and specifically his week. This sounds like the apocalypse of weeks given in the *Ancient book of Enoch, 91-93*. If so, we are missing some of the information.

Columns 10-12 relate Noah sacrificing after the flood. It records the names of his grandsons and the sacrifice he offered right before receiving the prophetic dream.

Columns 13-15 record the dream of Noah during the time referenced in Genesis 9:20-29. Noah sees himself as a great cedar tree. He is the king of the earth decreeing the Noahide laws for all nations. But the nations ignore him and one after another seek to conquer the world. Only Shem remains loyal to Noah and God, so Noah anoints him to be the new priest and a prophecy is given that "among his seed Your name will be called." This means the Messiah will be descended from Shem. Invasions come from the west (Canaan) and the North (Nimrod after he defeats Japheth's sons in a war). Column 15 advances into the end times with the Messiah bringing judgment from the southern part of the land and sealing all the rebels in the pit eternally.

Columns 16-18 recount the dividing of the earth between Noah's three sons and their subdivision of it. This same account appears in full in the *Ancient Book of Jubilees 8-9.*

Testament of Abraham

1Q20, cols. 19-22

Column 19

I called there on the name of God, saying, "You are God... King of Eternity." God spoke to me that night "... why wander? You have not reached the holy mountain." So, I traveled there. I went to the south around Moreh[i]... and continued until I came to Hebron. I built part of Hebron at that time and dwelt there for two years. A famine occurred over all this land; but, I heard that there was food in Egypt. I travelled toward the land of Egypt... until I reached the Carmon River, the last of seven streams that flow into the Great Salt Sea. I said to myself, "Now we are crossing into the land of the sons of Ham, the land of Egypt." The very first night we were in Egypt I had a dream.

In my dream, I saw a mountain with a cedar tree and a date palm, but they both had sprouted from the same root. Men came to cut down and uproot the cedar tree in order to separate it from the date palm. The date palm cried out, "Do not cut down the cedar, because we both grew from

---

[i] "Moreh" means teacher. This says he went around a place called Moreh. This may have been the yeshiva of Shem. It is a show of respect, if you are not going to a holy place to study or sacrifice, to travel around it.

the same root." So, they left the cedar alone on account the date palm, and did not cut it down.

Then I awoke terrified, and I said to my wife, Sarai, "I have had a horrible dream, and I am really afraid." She said to me, "Tell me your dream, so that I understand." I told the dream, then said to her, "This dream warns that there are those in Egypt who will kill me to get to you, so this is the kindness that you must do for me: if anyone asks you who I am, tell them; 'He is my brother.' In this way, you will protect me and my life will be spared. They will try to take you away from me, and even kill me if necessary." Sarai wept that night because of what I had said. When we entered Zoan, a district in Egypt, she was so concerned that no man should see her, that she concealed herself as best as she could. After five years, three men from the nobles of Egypt, servants of the Pharaoh of Zoan, were coming to me to hear my words of wisdom. They gave me gifts and asked advice about their personal lives, so I read to them out of the *Book of Enoch*...

Column 20

"...her face is irresistible and so beautiful; her forehead and soft flowing hair, her eyes, nose, every feature is prefect. She is a radiating beauty! And her breasts, oh, and her white complexion. Her arms and hands are perfect. Long, thin, and graceful hands and fingers. Her legs and feet are perfectly proportioned. She is more beautiful than any virgin or bride entering the bridal chamber. She is more beautiful than any woman I have ever seen; and in addition to that, she has great wisdom. Everything about her is absolutely prefect!" When the king heard everything Herqanos and his two companions said, he really wanted her.

He quickly sent someone to try to acquire her. When he saw her, he was completely dumbfounded by her beauty, and just had to have her for a wife. He also started to kill me, but Sarai told him that I was her bother, so I was spared because of her.

I, Abram, wept bitterly that night – I and Lot, my nephew, with me – when Sarai was forcefully taken away from me. I begged God for mercy that night. With tears running down my face, I prayed, "Blessed be the Most High God, Lord of all Ages, You are Lord and Ruler over all Creation. You rule over all the kings of the earth, and have the power to pass judgment on them. I cry out to You, my Lord. Pharaoh of Zoan, king of Egypt, has taken my wife away from me by force. Judge him for me. Reveal Your mighty hand to him and all his household. Please, do not let him defile my wife! This way they will all know that You, my Lord, are Lord over all the kings of the earth." I was so upset I just could not stop crying. But that night, the Most High God sent a spirit that caused a disease to afflict him and his entire household. He was not able to have sexual relations with her. The affliction was ongoing and after two years the disease grew much worse. So, he sent for all the wise men of Egypt, the magicians and physicians, to try to heal him and his household of this affliction. Not only could they not heal them, but they became infected as well and they all fled.

Then Herqanos came to me and asked if I would come lay hands on him and pray that he be healed. He asked this because he had seen this occur in a dream. But Lot interrupted him saying, "Abram, my uncle, cannot pray over the king while he holds his wife, Sarai, captive! Go tell the king to send Sarai back to her lawful husband. Only then can Abram pray over him.[j] If he hurries he *might* survive." When Hyrqanos heard what Lot said, he went and told the king, "The afflictions troubling my lord, the king, are due to Sarai. She is the *wife* of Abram. If you send Sarai back to her husband, the affliction of this putrid spirit will vanish."

So, the king called for me. When I came before him he said, "What have you done to me? Why did you tell me Sarai was your sister when she was really your wife? That is why I took her to be my wife! Here is your wife. Take her, go. Get out of Egypt! But before you go, pray over me and my household, so that this evil spirit will leave." I laid my hands on his head and prayed for his healing. Immediately the evil spirit left, and he and his household were restored to full health.

---

[j] The Lord used problems and illnesses to cause people to repent of their sins. We should only pray for non-believers to repent. We pray for healing and blessing for believers.

That same day the king gave me many gifts and swore an oath to me that he never had sexual relations with Sarai, or defiled her in any way. He gave her gold, silver, clothes of fine linen and purple, and a handmaid named Hagar. He then appointed an escort to take us back to the border of Egypt. Now I, Abram, left Egypt with a tremendous amount of flocks, silver, and gold. Lot, my brother's son, came with me. Lot had also acquired many flocks and took an Egyptian wife.

Column 21

I stopped at each of my former encampments until I arrived at Bethel, the place where I had built the altar. I then rebuilt it and offered up a burnt offering and a meal offering to the Most High God. There, I called on the name of the Lord of the Ages. I praised God, blessed Him, and thanked Him for all the flocks and wonderful things that He gave to me, and because He had kept me safe and returned me to this land in peace.

Later, Lot separated from me due to the behavior of our shepherds. I added to the flocks that he possessed and he left with them and headed toward the Jordan Valley. When he came to the city of Sodom, he bought a house there. He lived in Sodom while I was living in Bethel. I did not like that fact that Lot, my brother's son, was on his own.

Then God appeared to me in a dream, saying, "Go up to Ramat-Hazor, north of Bethel, where you now live. Lift up your eyes and look to the east, west, south, and north.

Testament of Abraham

The entire land that you view from there I will give to you and to your descendants for all ages."

In the morning I went up to Ramat-Hazor and I viewed the Land from its high point. I could see from the River of Egypt to Lebanon and Senir, and from the Great Sea to Hauran, and all the land of Gebal up to Kadesh, and the entire Great Desert east of Hauran and Senir, up to the Euphrates. He told me, "I will give all of this land to your descendants, as an inheritance for all ages. I will make them as numerous as the dust of the earth, uncountable. Go and walk the length and width of the land and see how great it is. I will give it to you and your descendants after you for all time."

So, I, Abram, surveyed the land. I traveled the circuit beginning at the Gihon River, and along the Sea to Mount Taurus. Then I traversed along the shore of the Great Salt Sea and alongside Mount Taurus to the east, through the entire breadth of the land, until I came to the Euphrates River. I journeyed along the Euphrates until I reached the Erythrean Sea, to the east, and went along that sea until I came to the gulf of the Red Sea, which joins the Erythrean Sea. I went through the south until I reached the Gihon River. Then I safely returned home to find all of my people were well. We moved from there to the Oaks of Mamre, which are slightly northeast of Hebron.

I built an altar there and offered a burnt offering and a meal offering to the Most High God. I ate and drank there with all my household. Then I sent an invitation to

Ancient Testaments of the Patriarchs

Mamre, Arnem, and Eshkol, three Amorite brothers, friends of mine, and they ate and drank with me.

Fourteen years earlier, Chedarlaomer, the king of Elam, Amraphel, the king of Babylon, Arioch, the king of Cappadocia, and Tiral, the king of Mesopotamian Goiim, came and waged war with Bera, the king of Sodom; Birsha, the king of Gomorrah; Shinab, the king of Admah; Shemiabad, the king of Zeboiim; and with the king of Bela. This battle was fought in the Valley of Siddim. The king of Elam and those with him were victorious over the king of Sodom and his allies. Chedarlaomer imposed tribute on them. They submitted to his authority and taxes for twelve years. They rebelled in the thirteenth year and in the fourteenth year Chedarlaomer amassed his army and went by way of the desert, destroying and plundering from the Euphrates River on. They destroyed the Rephaim in Ashtera, the Karnaim and the Zamzumim in Amman, the Emim, in Shaveh-Hakerioth, and the Hurrians in the mountains of Gebal. Then they came to El-Paran, in the desert. After camping there for a while they destroyed Ein-[Dina] in Hazazon-Tamar.

Now the king of Sodom, allied with the kings of Gomorrah, Admah, Zeboiim, and Bela, met Chedarlaomer's forces in battle in the Valley of Siddim. Chedarlaomer crushed the resistance. The king of Sodom fled, the king of Gomorrah and many others were killed. The king of Elam plundered all the goods of Sodom and

Gomorrah, including Lot, Abram's nephew, with all of his belongings.

Column 22

While Abram was eating and drinking with his friends Arnem, Eshkol, and Mamre, one of the shepherds Abram had given to Lot escaped and came to Abram who was living in Hebron. He told Abram about the battle and that Lot had been captured along with all his property, but Lot was still alive. He told Abram that Chedarlaomer had taken captives, plundered, destroyed, and murdered all the way through the Great Valley; and now his army was heading for Damascus. Abram wept for his nephew Lot. After he got himself together, he chose out of his servants three hundred and eighteen seasoned warriors. Arnem, Eshkol, and Mamre joined him. They followed the trail, and found the army resting in the Valley of Dan.

Abram's men attacked them at night from all four sides, killing them all through the night. He crushed the army, but many fled. Abram caught up to the remnant in Helbon, just north of Damascus. There he freed all their prisoners and gave everyone back their belongings. Lot, his nephew, was freed and got back all his property.

When the king of Sodom heard that Abram had brought back all the captives of his people and all their property, he went up to Salem, which is Jerusalem, to meet him. Abram was encamped in the Valley Shaveh, also called the Valley of the King – the Valley of Bet-Hakerem.

King Melchizedek of Salem brought out food and drink for Abram and all his men. He was the priest of the Most High God. Melchizedek blessed Abram, saying, "Blessed be Abram by the Most High God, the Lord of heaven and earth! Blessed be the Most High God, who delivered your enemies into your hands!" Then Abram gave him a tenth of all the property of the king of Elam and his allies to Melchizedek.

Then the king of Sodom came to Abram and said, "My lord, Abram, give me my citizens out of the prisoners whom you rescued from the king of Elam. You may take all the spoils."

Then Abram said to the king of Sodom, "I raise my hands and swear to the Most High God, the Lord of heaven and earth, that I will take none of the spoil that belonged to you. I do not want you to be able to say 'Abram is wealthy because he took my property as a spoil,' excluding the food my men have eaten and the portion of the three men who fought alongside me. Only they have authority to give you their portions. So Abram returned all the captives along with all the property to the king of Sodom. Every last one of the captives were freed and sent home.

After this, God appeared to Abram in a vision, and said to him, "Ten years have gone by since you left Haran; two years here, seven in Egypt, then one more after you returned from Egypt. Take an inventory of your possessions. They have more than doubled since you left

Testament of Abraham

Haran. Do not fear. I am with you, and will support and strengthen you. I will protect you from those who are stronger than you. Your wealth and property will increase enormously." Abram said, "My Lord God, I have great wealth and property, but what good are they if I die childless? One of my household servants, Eliezer of Damascus, will inherit all I have." But He said, "Eliezer will not receive your inheritance, but your biological child…"

Commentary

It is interesting to see God warn Abraham about Pharaoh taking Sarah for himself with deadly force. We should take warnings seriously but use good judgment.

Testament of Jacob

4Q537

Fragment 1
"...your descendants. All just and upright men will survive..., absolutely no deceit or debauchery is to be found... Now, take the tablets and read everything..." ... and all my troubles and all that was to happen to me over the one hundred and forty-seven years of my life. Again, he said to me, "Take the tablet from my hands..." So, I took the tablets from him... and I saw written in them that you would leave there on *that* day... corrupted before the Most High God.

Fragment 2
...and how the temple will be and how their priests will dress, and... their purification rites; how they will offer sacrifices on the altar; and how they will eat a part of their sacrifices as their food, in the whole land... who will leave the city and from under the walls; and where they will... before me a land of two quarter parts and...

Fragment 3
...of the land, and you will eat its fruit and all that is good, and you will live... to go insane and err, and to go in the path of the error of... your wickedness, until finally you will be to Him a...

Testament of Jacob

Commentary

The fragments of the *Testament of Jacob* seem to be saying that Jacob saw in a dream that his descendants would be enslaved in a foreign country and leave on a specific day (as Abraham had prophesied). They would enter the Promised Land, and some of them would become priests and work in a magnificent temple with underground passages holding amazing relics. The rituals those priests would perform were described to him. But, in time, the priesthood would become corrupt.

This testament of Jacob is described in Jubilees:

> 21. And he saw in a vision of the night, and behold an angel descended from heaven with seven tablets in his hands, and he gave them to Jacob, and he read them and knew all that was written therein which would befall him and his sons throughout all the ages. 22. He showed him all that was written on the tablets, and said unto him, "Do not build this place, and do not make it an eternal sanctuary, and do not dwell here; for this is not the place. Go to the house of Abraham your father and dwell with Isaac your father until the day of the death of your father. 23. For in Egypt you will die in peace, and in this land you will be buried with honor in the sepulcher of your fathers, with Abraham and Isaac. 24. Fear not, for

as you have seen and read it, thus will it all be; and write down everything as you have seen and read." 25. And Jacob said: "Lord, how can I remember all that I have read and seen?" He said unto him: "I will bring all things to your remembrance." 26. He went up from him, and he awoke from his sleep, and he remembered everything which he had read and seen, and he wrote down all the words which he had read and seen. *Ancient book of Jubilees 32:21-27*

Testament of Reuben

Concerning Thoughts

1. Reuben's Sin

The copy of the testament of Reuben and what things he charged his sons before he died in the hundred and twenty-fifth year of his life. When he was sick two years after the death of Joseph, his sons and grandsons gathered together to visit him. He told them, "My children, I am dying, and will go to my fathers." When he saw there Judah, Gad, and Asher, his brothers, he said to them, "Raise me up so I can tell you and my children what is in my heart." They got him up, then he kissed them, and said, tearfully, "Listen to me, your father, and follow my commands. I call the God of heaven to witness my words to you. Do not walk in the ignorance of youth and fornication like I did. I defiled the bed of my father, Jacob. For this, God gave me a disease in my loins that lasted seven months. If Jacob, our father, had not prayed for me, I know I would have died. I was thirty years old when I sinned in the sight of the Lord, and for seven months I was deathly sick; and I repented for seven years purposing in my heart before the Lord not to drink wine or strong drink nor eat meat or pleasant food, mourning over my sin. Such a great sin should never be seen in Israel."

2. The Eight Gifts

"Learn this lesson, my children. The time of my repentance has taught me that every man is born with eight gifts from God, but Belial twists them into seven errors, which are mainly done in youth.

1. Life, by which man's whole being is created;
2. Sight, which arouses desire;
3. Hearing, which brings learning;
4. Smell and taste, which is given by breath;
5. Speech, which brings knowledge;
6. Taste, which turns food and drink into strength;
7. Reproduction and sexual desire, with which, through love of pleasure, sin also enters in. Therefore, it is the last in order of creation, and the first of youth, because it is filled with ignorance, which leads the young as a blind man to a pit.
8. Dreams, which create entrancement of man's nature, and the image of death.

3. The Eight Sins

"When these eight gifts are mingled with error they create:

1. Fornication, which dwells in our nature and senses;
2. Gluttony and drunkenness;
3. Fighting, in the liver and the gall;
4. Deceit and trickery, that through over-aggressiveness a man may seem fair;
5. Arrogance, that a man may be stirred up and become high-minded;

6. Lying with jealousy, to deceive or hide the truth;
7. Injustice, which brings theft. When combined with other errors beings craft;
8. Dreams with error and fantasy, which destroys a young man by darkening his mind from truth, God's law, and the warnings of his fathers.

"My children, love truth and it will preserve you. Listen to my counsel. Do not take a woman just for her outward beauty, privately associate with a married woman, or meddle in a woman's affairs. For if I had not seen Bilhah bathing in a private place, I would not have committed this great sin. I could not stop seeing her nakedness in my mind. I couldn't sleep. I just had to have her. So, when Jacob and Isaac went away, and we were at Gader, near Bethlehem Ephratha, Bilhah was drunk, and asleep naked in her tent. I went in to her tent and saw her lying naked, I committed the sin, then left her lying there asleep. An angel of God revealed my sin to my father, Jacob, and he came and mourned over me, and touched her no more.

4. Fornication

"Pay no attention to the beautiful women, and do not even be involved with them; but walk with the Lord with a pure heart and in fear. Work, study, and focus on your flocks, until the Lord gives to you the wife He wants you to have, so that you will not suffer as I did. Until my father's death I was never bold enough to look him in the eye, or stand up to my brothers, because of my reproach. Even now my conscience bothers me because of my sin. My father forgave me; he prayed for my forgiveness and healing. From that point on, I was protected, and I never committed that sin again. Therefore, my children, observe all my commands, and you will not fall into sin. Fornication destroys the soul, separates you from God, and entices you into idolatry, because it deceives your mind and understanding and will lead you to Hell before your time. Belial has destroyed many through fornication; even noble elderly men have ruined their lives because of it. Joseph kept himself from every woman, and purged his thoughts from all fornication. He found favor before the Lord and men. For the Egyptian woman did many things unto him, and called for magicians, and offered him love potions, but he purposed in his soul not to allow the evil desire. Therefore, God kept him from death. If fornication does not overcome your mind, neither will Belial overcome you.

5. Modest Dress

My children, ungodly women hurt you, not by strength, but by subtle enticement. They hide who they really are and make you see what they want you to see. They cannot overcome you by strength, so they overcome you by craft. An angel of God told me that fornication overcomes ungodly women more than men. They devise schemes to seduce men; they deceive a man's mind through their adornment, instill poison by the glance of their eye, and capture him by their actions. Therefore, flee fornication, my children. Command your wives and daughters not to adorn their heads and faces; because every woman who acts deceitfully in these things is destined for everlasting punishment. This is how they seduced the Watchers

Testament of Reuben

before the flood; they appeared constantly in their presence this way until the watchers fell for them. They changed their form into that of men and came to the women. The ungodly women planned for this to happen because they desired heavenly husbands. Then they gave birth to Nephilim.

6. Levi's Priesthood

"Beware of fornication; and if you wish to have a pure mind, guard your senses against every woman. Command your wives and daughters not to keep company with men, so that they will also keep their minds pure.[k] Even if they do not fornicate, constant meetings are an incurable disease to women, and an everlasting reproach of Belial to men. He who is wise and godly will not fall into fornication; neither will he who controls his desires fall into jealousy. Therefore, you will be jealous against the sons of Levi, and will seek to be exalted over them; but you will fail, because God will avenge them. You will die an evil death. For the Lord made Levi, Judah, Dan, Joseph, and me rulers over you. Therefore, I command you to obey Levi, because he will know the law of the Lord, and will create ordinances for judgment and sacrifice for all Israel until the time of Messiah, the High Priest whom the Lord has declared. I adjure you by the God of heaven to be truthful to each other; and humbly submit to Levi, that you may receive his blessing. For he will bless Israel; and specially Judah, because the Lord

---

[k] Courtship, not dating.

chose him to rule over all the people. We will worship his Seed, because He will die for us in wars visible and invisible, and will be among you an everlasting king."

7. Reuben's Death
Reuben died after giving these commands to his sons; and they placed him in a coffin until they brought him up from Egypt, and buried him in Hebron in the double cave where his fathers are.

Commentary
Reuben 6 gives a prophecy that Levi would obtain the priesthood until the Messiah arises from the tribe of Judah. This Messiah will be a man, but also God incarnate. He will die for us and yet rule forever. He will be worshiped as God incarnate by all true believers. The Apostle Paul described a law which was added until Messiah came, in Galatians 3:16-17. Reuben teaches here the "temporary law" was that which was the ordinances for judgment and sacrifice created by Levi and the priesthood.

Testament of Simeon

Concerning Envy

1. Simeon

The copy of the words of Simeon, what things he spoke to his sons before he died, in the hundred and twentieth year of his life, in the year in which Joseph died. For they came to visit him when he was sick, and he strengthened himself and sat up and kissed them, and said to them:

2. Simeon's Heart

Listen, my children, to what is on my heart. I was Jacob's second son. My mother, Leah, called me Simeon, because the Lord heard her prayer.[1] I became very strong. I took unnecessary risks because I was afraid of nothing. I allowed myself to become hard-hearted, stubborn, and uncompassionate because the Most High endowed me with bravery. I became jealous of my brother Joseph simply because my father loved him. I allowed the Prince of Deceit to so overwhelm my mind with jealousy that I decided to kill my own brother. I never once thought about how it would affect my father, Jacob. God delivered him from me. When I went to buy ointment for the flock and Reuben went to Dotham for other supplies our brother, Judah, sold him to the Ishmaelites. Reuben was grieved, for he wished to restore Joseph safe to his

---

[1] Genesis 29:33

father.ᵐ But I was furious with Judah because he let Joseph live. I was so wrathful I plotted against Judah and God punished me. I lost the use of my right hand. That brought me to my senses and I repented for seven days. I prayed that the Lord would restore the use of my hand and keep me from falling back into the sin of envy and all foolishness. I knew this was the punishment for my envy against my bother Joseph.

3. Flee Envy
My children, guard yourselves against the deceit of envy. It takes over your mind so that you cannot eat, drink, or do any good. Envy destroys the one who envies, but the one who is envied always flourishes. After praying and fasting, I realized envy is only overcome by the by the fear of God. If you flee to the Lord, envy ceases and your mind rests. You are able to sympathize with the one you envied and become one of those who love him.

4. Avoid Jealousy and Envy
When we went down into Egypt, and he bound me as a spy, I knew that I deserved it, and I did not grieve. Joseph was a good man, and had the Spirit of God within him. Compassionate and pitiful, he did not bare any malice against me. He loved me and the rest of his brothers.

My children, avoid all jealousy and envy. Live a devoted life with a good heart, so that God will bless you like He

---

ᵐ Genesis 37:22, 29; 42:22

did Joseph. Joseph never brought up the incident. Instead he loved us and gave us great riches. Love each other and forsake envy because it ruins both the soul and body. It turns anger to war and puts you in a frenzy so that you cannot sleep. It destroys your wisdom, gnaws at your soul, stresses the body, and brings confusion. You actually begin to look like your body has been poisoned.

5. Be Righteous and Study Prophecy

Joseph was so good looking because he did not poison his body with wicked intentions. You can always see this in a person's face. My children be righteous before God and you will find favor with both God and men. Do not fornicate; it is the mother of all evils. It separates you from God, and pushes you toward Belial. I have seen in the writing of Enoch that your sons will be corrupted by fornication and will attack Levi with the sword. But Levi will win the war of the Lord, and will conquer all of you. Levi and Judah will always produce the true kings and priests and rule over you as our father Jacob has prophesied.

6. Prophecy will be Fulfilled!

I have foretold you all these things to make myself clear about the sin of your souls. If you forsake envy and stubbornness, you will flourish like a rose, like the cedars of Lebanon, and you will be holy forever, and will branch afar off. Then the seed of Canaan, Amalek, the

Philistines,[n] the Hittites, and all the cursed seed of Ham will perish. Then the world will rest from war and Shem will be glorified, because the Lord God, the Mighty One of Israel, will appear upon earth as man, and save the seed of Adam. Then all the deceitful, wicked, spirits will be trampled underfoot, and no longer rule over man. Then will I arise [at the Resurrection] in joy, and will bless the Most High because of His marvelous works, because God hath taken a body and eaten with men and saved men.

7. The Messiah

My children, obey Levi, and in Judah will you be redeemed. Do not rebel against these two tribes, for from them will arise the salvation of God. For the Lord will raise up from Levi as it were a Priest,[o] and from Judah as it were a King, who is both God and man. So, He will save all the Gentiles and Israel. Therefore, I command you these things, in order that you also may command your children, that they may observe them throughout their generations.

8. Simeon's Death and Burial

Simeon finished speaking, and died, being a hundred and twenty years old. They laid him in a wooden coffin and took his remains to be buried in Hebron about the time of the Egyptian war (with the Philistines). They did this secretly because the bones of Joseph and his brothers

---

[n] Lit. Cappadocians. Compare Deuteronomy 2:23 LXX and Amos 9:7 LXX
[o] John the Baptist

Testament of Simeon

were guarded in the treasure-house of Egypt; for the sorcerers told them that when the bones of Joseph leave Egypt there would be such a great darkness throughout all the land that a man will not be able to see his brother even with a lamp.

9. The Wait till Moses

The sons of Simeon mourned for their father according to the law, and they continued living in Egypt until the day of their departure by the hand of Moses.

Commentary

Simeon 5 teaches that Enoch predicted a civil war in Israel and stated that Jacob was a prophet.

Simeon 6 teaches that Levi has the priesthood and Judah has the kingship. In time, the Canaanites will be wiped out and the Messiah (the God-man) will come to earth and bring salvation for all mankind. After this, the resurrection will occur.

Simeon 7 also mentions that the Messiah will be both God and man.

Testament of Levi

Concerning the Priesthood and Arrogance.

1. Levi
The copy of the words of Levi to his sons, including his commands and prophecies. He was in good health when he called them to him, for it had been shown to him that he should die. When they were gathered together he said to them:

2. Levi's First Dream
I, Levi, was born in Haran. When I was young my father moved us to Shechem. When I was about twenty, Simeon and I took vengeance on Hamor for our sister Dinah. One day we were feeding our flocks in Abel-Maul, and the spirit of understanding of the Lord came upon me, and I understood that all men corrupt their way, and that righteousness had retreated behind walls and iniquity ruled. I grieved for mankind, and I prayed to the Lord that I might be saved.

Then I fell asleep, and I beheld a high mountain. It was Aspis in Abel-Maul. The heavens opened, and an angel of God said to me, "Levi, enter." I travelled into the first and then into the second heaven. There was a body of water between them. When I came to the third heaven it was far brighter than the first two, and its height was without bounds. I asked the angel, "why is the third heaven brighter than the first two?" The angel replied, "You will see four other heavens brighter than these, without comparison. For you will stand before the Lord, be His minister, reveal the redeemer of Israel,[p] and His mysteries to men. The Lord will appear among men through you and Judah, saving them out of every race. Serving the Lord will be your portion in life.

3. Seven Heavens Explained

"Listen concerning the seven heavens.[q] The lowest is darker because it is near all the iniquities of men. The second has fire, snow, and ice, ready for the day of the Lord, when the righteous judgment of God is poured out in vengeance on the wicked. In the third are the hosts of the armies which are ordained for the day of judgment, to work vengeance on the spirits of deceit and of Belial. The top four heavens are holy, for in the highest of all dwells the Great Glory, in the holy of holies, far above all holiness. In the sixth are the angels of the presence of the Lord, who minister and make propitiation to the Lord for all the sins the righteous committed in ignorance; and they offer to the Lord a reasonable sweet-smelling savor, and a bloodless offering. In the fifth heaven are the angels who bear the answers to the angels of the presence of the Lord. And in the fourth heaven are thrones and dominions, in which hymns are ever offered to God. Therefore, whenever the Lord looks upon us, all of us

---

[p] Luke 24:21
[q] For the Jewish idea of seven heavens, cf. Clement of Alexandra, Strom., iv. 7; and Paul in the third heaven in 2 Corinthians 12:2.

tremble. The heavens, the earth, and the abysses tremble in the presence of His majesty; but the sons of men who do not regard these things, sin, and provoke the Most High.

4. Levi Forgiven, and the Messiah's Coming

Understand that the Lord will execute judgment upon the sons of men; because when the rocks are rent,[r] the sun quenched, the waters dried up, the fire trembling, all creation troubled, the invisible spirits melting away, and the grave spoiled in the suffering of the Most High, unbelieving men will continue in their iniquity. Therefore, they will be judged. The Most High has heard your prayer. Your sins are forgiven, and you will become a son to Him, a servant and minister of His presence. You will shine the light of knowledge to Jacob, a sun to the seed of Israel. You and all your seed will be blessed until the Lord visits all the heathen in the tender mercies of His Son, even forever. Nevertheless, your sons will lay hands upon Him to crucify Him. Therefore, you have been given counsel and understanding to instruct your sons about Him, because he who blesses Him will be blessed, but they that curse Him will perish."[s]

5. The Command to Destroy Shechem

Then the angel opened the gates of heaven, and I saw the holy temple, and the Most High upon a throne of glory. He said to me, "Levi, I have given you the blessings of

---

[r] Matthew 27:51
[s] Genesis 12:3

Testament of Levi

the priesthood until I will come and sojourn in the midst of Israel." Then the angel brought me to the earth, and gave me a shield and a sword, and said, "Take vengeance on Shechem because of Dinah, and I will be with you, because the Lord has sent me." In the dream, I destroyed the sons of Hamor, like the heavenly tablets recorded that I would. I asked the angel to tell me his name, so I could call on him in the day of tribulation. He said to me, "I am the angel who intercedes for the children of Israel, that He not totally destroy them, because every evil spirit attacks them." Then I awoke from the dream and blessed the Most High and the angel who intercedes for the children of Israel and all the righteous.

6. Destruction of Shechem

When I came to my father, I found a brazen shield. Therefore, the name of the mountain is called Aspis. It is near Gebal, on the right side of Abila; and I kept these things in my heart. I suggested to my father and my brother, Reuben, that he should bid the sons of Hamor to be circumcised. I was indignant because of the abomination which they had done in Israel. First, I killed Shechem and then Simeon killed Hamor. After that, our brothers came and attacked the city with the edge of the sword. Our father heard it and was very angry, and he was grieved that they were put to death after they were circumcised. He still blessed us, but it was a sin because we did this without his knowledge, and he was sick all that day. But I knew that this was the proper sentence that God passed on Shechem; for they had tried to do to the same thing to Sarah as they did to Dinah our sister, but the Lord hindered them. Not only that, but they persecuted Abraham our father when he lived near there by shamefully harassing his flocks, shepherds, and Jeblae, his servant, who was born in his house. This is what they did to all strangers, taking away their wives by force, and exiling the men. But the wrath of the Lord hit them suddenly and completely.

7. Jacob's Anger Soothed

I said to my father, "Sir, please do not be not angry. The Lord will destroy all the Canaanites and give the entire land to your descendants. From this day forward Shechem will be called *a city of those who are without understanding*; for as a man mocks a fool, we mocked them, because they wrought folly in Israel by defiling our sister." We took our sister and went back to Bethel.

8. Second Vision – The Three Priesthoods

<u>After seventy days, while at Bethel, I dreamed again like the former dream. I saw seven men in white raiment saying to me, "Arise[t],</u> put on the robe of the priesthood, the crown of righteousness, the breastplate of understanding, the garment of truth, the diadem of faith, the crown of miracles, and the ephod of prophecy." Each one of them gave me one of these things. I put them on and then they said, "From now on you are a priest of the Lord, you and your seed forever." The first anointed me with holy oil, and gave to me the rod of judgment. The

---

[t] 4Q213b

Testament of Levi

second washed me with pure water, and fed me with bread and wine, the most holy things, and dressed me with a holy and glorious robe. The third clothed me with a linen garment like an ephod. The fourth put around me a purple girdle. The fifth gave me a branch of rich olive. The sixth placed a crown on my head. The seventh placed on my head a diadem of priesthood, and filled my hands with incense, so that I served as a priest to the Lord. They said to me, "Levi, your seed will be divided into three branches,[u] for a sign of the glory of the Lord who is to come.

- The first will be he who has been faithful; no portion will be greater than his.
- The second will be in the priesthood.
- The third—a new name will be called over Him, because He will arise as King from Judah, and will establish a new priesthood, after the fashion of the Gentiles, to all the Gentiles.[v] His appearing will be unutterable, as of an exalted prophet of the seed of Abraham our father.

Every desirable thing in Israel will be for you and for your seed, and everything fair to look upon will you eat, and the table of the Lord your seed will apportion, and some of them will be high priests, judges, and scribes; for by their mouth will the holy place be guarded." When I

---

[u] Moses (Law), Aaron (Priesthood) and Jesus (Melchizedek)
[v] Noahide Law with a Noahide / Melchizedekian Priesthood

awoke, I understood that this dream was like the former dream. I hid this also in my heart, and did not tell anyone.

9. Levi Learns the Priesthood

After two days Judah and I went up to Isaac after our father; and my grandfather blessed me according to all the words of the visions which I had seen. He would not come with us to Bethel. When we came to Bethel, my father Jacob had a vision concerning me, that I should become a priest unto the Lord; and he rose up early in the morning, and paid tithes of all to the Lord through me. We came to Hebron to dwell there, and Isaac continually taught me the law of the Lord, even as the angel of God showed to me.[w] He taught me the law of the priesthood, of sacrifices, whole burnt-offerings, first-fruits, free-will offerings, and thank-offerings. Every day he instructed me, and prayed for me before the Lord. He told me, "Take heed, my child, of the spirit of fornication;[x] for this will continue, and will by your seed pollute the holy things. Therefore, while yet you are still young, take a wife, without blemish, nor yet polluted, nor of the race of the Philistines or Gentiles. Before entering into the holy place, bathe; and when you offer the sacrifice, wash; and again, when you finish the sacrifice, wash. Of twelve evergreen trees, offer up the fruits to the Lord, as Abraham taught me. Of every clean beast and clean bird

---

[w] 4Q213b
[x] Idolatry

offer a sacrifice to the Lord. Of every firstling and of wine offer first-fruits. Every sacrifice you will salt with salt." [y]

10. Levi to His Children

My children, observe my commands. I have explained to you what I have learned from my fathers. I am clear from all your ungodliness and transgression which you will do in the end of the ages against the Savior of the world, acting ungodly, deceiving Israel, and raising up against it great evils from the Lord. You will deal lawlessly with Israel, so that Jerusalem will not endure your wickedness; but the veil of the temple will be rent, so as not to cover your shame. You will be scattered as captives among the heathen, and will be for a reproach, for a curse, and for a trampling under foot. For the house which the Lord will choose will be called Jerusalem, as is contained in the book of Enoch the Righteous.

11. Levi's Children

Therefore, I took Melcha as a wife when I was twenty-eight years old. She called our firstborn son Gersham, because we were sojourners in our land. Gersham means "sojourning." But I saw that he should not inherit the blessing of the firstborn. Kohath was born in my thirty-fifth year, towards the east. Later, in a vision, I saw him standing high above all the congregation. Therefore, I called his name Kohath, which means, beginning of majesty and instruction. Thirdly, she bore Merari, in the

---

[y] 4Q214, 4Q214b

<u>fortieth year of my life</u>[z]; and since his mother bare him with difficulty, she called him Merari, which means "my bitterness," because he also died. <u>Jochebed was born in my sixty-fourth year</u>,[aa] in Egypt, for I was renowned then in the midst of my brothers.

12. Levi's Grandchildren

Gersham took a wife, and she gave birth to Lomni and Semei. The sons of Kohath were Amram, Isaar, Chebro, and Ozel. The sons of Merari were Mooli and Homusi. In my ninety-fourth year Amram took Jochebed my daughter to him to wife, for they were both born on the same day. Eight years old was I when I went into the land of Canaan, and eighteen years when I slew Shechem. At nineteen years, I became priest, and at twenty-eight years I took a wife. At forty years, I went into Egypt. Behold, you are my children and grandchildren. In my hundred and eighteenth year Joseph died.

13. Simplicity

Now, my children, I command you that you fear our Lord with your whole heart, and walk in simplicity according to all His law. Instruct your children so that they will understand all their life, reading unceasingly the law of God; for everyone who will know the law of God will be honored, and will not be a stranger wherever he goes. He will gain more friends than his forefathers did. Many men will desire to serve him, and to hear the law from him.

---

[z] 4Q214a, Fragments. 2-3
[aa] 4Q214a, Fragments. 4-6

Testament of Levi

Work righteousness, my children, upon the earth, that you may find treasure in heaven, and sow good things in your souls, that you may find them in your life. For if you sow evil things, you will reap all trouble and affliction. Get wisdom in the fear of God with diligence; for though there will be a captivity, cities destroyed, and lands, gold, silver, and every possession will perish, no one can take your wisdom from you! Ungodliness leads to blindness and sin. The wise will make friends of his enemies even in a foreign country. If a man teaches and practices these things, he will rule with kings, as Joseph our brother did.

14. The Corruption of the Levitical Priesthood

Now, my children, I have learned from the writing of Enoch that at the last you will deal ungodly, laying your hands on the Lord in all malice. Your brothers will be ashamed because of you, and all the Gentiles will mock you. Our father, Israel, will be pure from the ungodliness of the priests who will lay their hands upon the Savior of the world. Pure is the heaven above the earth, and you are the lights of the heaven as the sun and the moon. What will all the Gentiles do if you are darkened in ungodliness? You will bring a curse upon our race for whom the light of the world came, which was given among you for the lighting up of every man. You will desire to slay Him, teaching commandments contrary to the ordinances of God. The offerings of the Lord you will rob, and from His portion you will steal. Before you sacrifice to the Lord, you will take the choicest parts, in despitefulness eating them with harlots. Amid excesses you will teach the commandments of the Lord. The women that have husbands you will pollute, and the virgins of Jerusalem you will defile. With harlots and adulteresses you will be joined. The daughters of the Gentiles you will take for wives, purifying them with an unlawful purification; and your union will be like unto Sodom and Gomorrah in ungodliness. You will be prideful because of the priesthood, lifting yourselves up against men. Not only so, but being puffed up also against the commands of God, you will scoff at the holy things, mocking in despitefulness.

15. Roman Expulsion

Therefore, the temple which the Lord will choose will be desolate in uncleanness, and you will be captives throughout all nations. You will be an abomination among them, and you will receive reproach and everlasting shame from the righteous judgment of God. All who see you will flee from you. Were it not for God's promises to Abraham, Isaac, and Jacob, our fathers, not one from my seed should be left upon the earth.

16. Enoch's Prophecy

I have also learned in the book of Enoch that for seventy weeks you will go astray, will profane the priesthood, pollute the sacrifices, corrupt the law, and ignore the words of the prophets. In perverseness, you will persecute righteous men, hate the godly, and abhor the words of the faithful. The man who renews the law in the power of the

Most High you will call a deceiver.[bb] At last, as you suppose, you will slay Him, not understanding His resurrection, wickedly taking upon your own heads the innocent blood.[cc] Because of Him will your holy places be desolate, polluted even to the ground, and you will have no place that is clean; but you will be among the Gentiles a curse and a dispersion, until He will again look on you, and in pity will take you to Himself through faith and water.[dd]

17. Jubilees

Because you have heard concerning the seventy weeks, hear also concerning the priesthood. In each jubilee, there will be a priesthood.

- In the first jubilee, the first who is anointed into the priesthood will be great, and will speak to God as to a Father. His priesthood will be filled with the fear of the Lord, and in the day of his gladness will he arise for the salvation of the world.
- In the second jubilee, he who is anointed will be conceived in the sorrow of beloved ones. His priesthood will be honored, and will be glorified among all.
- The third priest will be held fast in sorrow;
- and the fourth will be in grief, because unrighteousness will be laid upon him exceedingly, and all Israel will hate each one his neighbor.

[bb] Matthew 27:63
[cc] Matthew 27:25
[dd] A return of the Levitical Priesthood?

- The fifth will be held fast in darkness, likewise also the sixth and the seventh.
- In the seventh there will be such pollution as I am not able to express, before the Lord and men, for they will know it who do these things. Therefore, they will be in captivity and for a prey, and their land and their substance will be destroyed. In the fifth week they will return into their desolate country, and will renew the house of the Lord.
- In the seventh week the priests will come, worshippers of idols, contentious, lovers of money, proud, lawless, lascivious, abusers of children and beasts.[ee]

18. Messiah's Priesthood

After the Lord punishes them, He will raise up to the priesthood a new Priest, to whom all the words of the Lord will be revealed. He will execute a judgment of truth upon the earth in the fullness of days. His star will arise in heaven, as a king shedding forth the light of knowledge in the sunshine of day, and He will be magnified in the world until His ascension. He will shine forth as the sun in the earth, and will drive away all darkness from the world under heaven, and there will be peace in all the earth. The heavens will rejoice in His days, the earth will be glad, and the clouds will be joyful. The knowledge of the Lord will be poured forth upon the earth, as the water of seas; and the angels of the glory of the presence of the

---

[ee] Priesthood becomes more and more corrupt till virtually no real priesthood exists in the 8-10 jubilees, when the Messiah comes.

Lord will be glad in Him. The heavens will be opened, and from the temple of glory will the sanctification come upon Him with the Father's voice, as from Abraham, the father of Isaac. The glory of the Most High will be uttered over Him, and the Spirit of understanding and of sanctification will rest upon Him in the water. He will give the majesty of the Lord to His sons in truth for evermore; and there will none succeed Him for all generations, even forever. In His priesthood the Gentiles will be multiplied in knowledge on the earth and enlightened through the grace of the Lord. In His priesthood all sin will come to an end, the lawless will rest from evil, and the just will rest in Him. He will open the gates of paradise, and will remove the threatening sword against Adam. He will give to His saints to eat from the tree of life, and the Spirit of holiness will be on them. Belial will be bound by Him, and He will give power to His children to tread upon the evil spirits. The Lord will rejoice in His children, and will be well pleased in His beloved forever. Then Abraham, Isaac, and Jacob will be joyful, and I will be glad, and all the saints will put on gladness.

19. Levi's Death

My children, you have heard everything. Choose for yourselves darkness or light; either the law of the Lord or the works of Belial. We swore to our father that before the Lord we will walk according to His law. Our father said, "The Lord and His angels are witnesses, as I am and you also, concerning your oath." We said, "We are witnesses." Levi ceased giving charge, laid down, and died, after he had lived a hundred and thirty-seven years. Then they laid him in a coffin, and afterwards buried him in Hebron, beside Abraham, Isaac, and Jacob.

Commentary

Levi 4 teaches that the Son of God will bring salvation but the sons of Levi will destroy (crucify) Him.

Levi 5 states that Levi has the priesthood until the Messiah comes.

Levi 8 teaches there will be three priesthoods. The Messiah, a descendant of Judah, will fashion a new Gentile-type priesthood.

Levi 10 predicts that at the end of the age the Messiah will come and the Levites will turn on Him, the veil in the temple will be torn in two. That chapter also teaches that Enoch prophesied about the Jerusalem temple.

Levi 14 says Enoch taught that the priests will turn on the Messiah.

Levi 16 reveals Enoch taught a seventy-weeks prophecy.

Levi 17 maps out the priesthood's fall into corruption in jubilee periods, starting with the Maccabees renewal to its complete corruption under the Romans. See the chapter on the *Prophecy Outline* for details.

Levi 18 mentions the Messiah's priesthood, ascension, baptism, spiritual gifts, and sanctification.

Testament of Judah

Concerning Fortitude, and Love of Money, and Fornication.

1. Judah

The copy of the words of Judah, which he spoke to his sons before he died: they gathered together around him, and he said, "I was my father's fourth son. My mother named me Judah, saying, 'I give thanks to the Lord, because He has given a fourth son to me.' I was swift and active in my youth, and obedient to my father in everything. I honored my mother and my mother's sister. When I grew up, my father, Jacob, prayed over me, saying, 'You will be a king, and prosper in all things.'

2. Judah's Strength and Cunning

"The Lord showed me favor in all my works both in the field and at home. When I saw that I could run with the hind, then I caught it, and prepared meat for my father. I seized upon the roes in the chase, and all that was in the plains I outran. A wild mare I outran, and I caught it and tamed it. I killed a lion, and plucked a kid out of its mouth. I took a bear by its paw, and rolled it over a cliff. If any beast turned upon me, I killed it like a dog. I encountered the wild boar, and overtaking it in the chase, I tore it. A leopard in Hebron leaped upon the dog, and I caught it by the tail, and flung it from me, and it was dashed to pieces in the coasts of Gaza. A wild ox feeding in the field I seized by the horns; and whirling it round and stunning it, I cast it from me, and killed it.

3. Canaanite Wars

"When the two kings of the Canaanites came in warlike array against our flocks, and many people with them, I, by myself, rushed upon King Sur and seized him; and I beat him upon the legs, and dragged him down, and killed him. The other king, Taphue, I killed as he sat upon his horse, and so I scattered all the people. King Achor, a man of giant stature, hurling darts before and behind as he sat on horseback, I killed; for I hurled a stone of sixty pounds, and cast it upon his horse, and killed him. I fought with Achor for two hours, and I killed him. I split his shield in two, and chopped off his feet. As I stripped off his breastplate, behold, eight of his companions began to fight with me. I used my garment as a sling and killed four of them. The rest fled. Jacob, my father, killed Beelisa, king of all the kings, a giant in strength, twelve cubits high. Fear fell on them, and they ceased from making war with us. Therefore, my father had no care in the wars when I was among my brothers. For he saw in a vision concerning me, that an angel of might followed me everywhere that I should not be overcome.

4. War in Hebron

"In the south, we faced a greater war than that in Shechem. I joined in the battle with my brothers, and pursued a thousand men. I killed two hundred of them and four kings. I went up against them on the wall, and killed two other kings; and so, we freed Hebron, and took all the captives of the kings.

5. Areta, Thaffu Destroyed
"On the next day, we departed to Areta, a strong, walled, and inaccessible city that threatened us with death. Therefore, Gad and I approached on the east side of the city, and Reuben and Levi on the west and south. Those who were upon the wall thought that we were alone, and charged down upon us. Our brothers secretly climbed up the wall on both sides by ladders, and entered into the city, while the men did not know it. We took it with the edge of the sword. We set fire to the tower, and took both it and those who had taken refuge there. As we were departing, the men of Thaffu set upon our captives. We and our sons fought with them even to Thaffu. We killed them, and burnt their city, and spoiled all the things that were in it.

6. Jobel and Machir Destroyed
"When I was at the waters of Chuzeba, the men of Jobel came to battle against us, and we fought with them. We killed their allies from Selom, and we allowed them no means of escaping or of coming against us. The men of Machir came on the fifth day to carry away our captives. We attacked them, and overcame them in fierce battle, for they were a mighty host in themselves. We killed them before they had gone up the side of the hill. When we came to their city, their women rolled stones on us from the brow of the hill on which the city stood. Simeon and I

hid ourselves behind the town, and seized the heights, and utterly destroyed the whole city.

7. More Canaanite Wars

"The next day we were told that the cities of the two kings with a great host were coming against us. Therefore, Dan and I feigned ourselves to be Amorites, and went as allies into their city. In the middle of the night our brothers came, and we opened the gates for them. We destroyed all the men and their substance, and we took for a spoil all that was theirs. We knocked down three of their walls. We drew near Thamna, where all the hostile kings took refuge. Having been injured I was angry, and chased them to the top of the hill. They shot stones and darts at me. If Dan my brother had not helped me, they would have been able to kill me. Therefore, we fiercely attacked them, and they all fled. Going around another way, they sought out my father, and he made peace with them. Therefore, we did them no harm, but made a truce with them, and restored to them all the captives. I built Thamna, and my father built Rhambael. I was twenty years old when this war happened, and the Canaanites feared me and my brothers.

8. Judah's Wife and Children

"Moreover, I had many cattle, and the chief of my herdsmen was Hirah the Adullamite. When I went to him, I saw Barsan, king of Adullam, who made us a feast. He entreated me, and gave me his daughter Bathshua for a wife. She bore me Er, Onan, and Shelah. The Lord struck two of them and they died childless, but Shelah lived, and you are his children.

9. Esau Slain

"For eighteen years after we came from Laban in Mesopotamia we and our father lived in peace with his brother Esau and his sons. After this, in the fortieth year of my life, Esau came against us with many strong people. He fell by the bow of Jacob,[ff] and was taken up dead in Mount Seir. As he went above Iramna he was slain. We pursued the sons of Esau. They had a city with walls of iron and gates of brass. We could not enter it, so we encamped around it, and besieged them. When they did not open to us after twenty days, I set up a ladder in the sight of all. With my shield on my head I climbed up, assailed with stones of three talents' weight. I climbed up, and killed four mighty men. The next day Reuben and Gad entered in and killed sixty others. Then they asked for terms of peace. Being aware of our father's purpose, we received them as tributaries. They gave us two hundred cors of wheat, five hundred baths of oil, and fifteen hundred measures of wine, until we went down into Egypt.

[ff] Jubilees 38 has the same story but the Talmud and Jasher tell a different story of Esau's death. One of the texts is corrupted. Most likely one deals with Esau's death and the other deals with the death of one of Esau's sons.

10. Tamar

"After these things, my son Er took to wife Tamar, from Mesopotamia, a daughter of Aram. Now Er was wicked, and he doubted concerning Tamar, because she was not of the land of Canaan. On the third night, an angel of the Lord killed him, because he had not known her, according to the evil craftiness of his mother, for he did not wish to have children from her. In the days of the wedding feast I espoused Onan to her. He also in wickedness refused to know her, though he lived with her a year. When I threatened him, he lay with her, but he did the way his mother told him, and he also died in his wickedness. I wanted to give Shelah to her also, but my wife, Bathshua, would not allow it; for she hated Tamar, because she was not of the daughters of Canaan, as she herself was.

11. Shelah

"I knew that the race of Canaan was wicked, but the thoughts of youth blinded my heart. When I saw Bathshua pouring out wine, in the drunkenness of wine was I deceived, and I fell in love with her. While I was away, she went and took for Shelah a wife from the land of Canaan. When I realized what she had done, I cursed her in the anguish of my soul, and she also died in the wickedness of her sons.

12. Judah sleeps with Tamar

"After these things, while Tamar was a widow, she heard after two years that I was going up to shear my sheep; then she decked herself in bridal array, and sat by the gate of the city. For it is a law of the Amorites, that she who is about to marry sit in fornication seven days by the gate. I therefore, being drunk at the waters of Chozeb, recognized her not by reason of wine; and her beauty deceived me, through the fashion of her adorning. I turned aside to her, and said, I would enter in to you. She said to me, 'What will you give me?' I gave her my staff, and my girdle, and my royal crown; and I lay with her, and she conceived. I then, not knowing what she had done, wished to slay her; but she secretly sent my pledges, and put me to shame. When I called her, I heard also the secret words which I spoke when lying with her in my drunkenness; and I could not slay her, because it was from the Lord. For I said, in case by accident she did it in subtlety, and received the pledge from another woman: but I came near her no more till my death, because I had done this abomination in all Israel. Moreover, they who were in the city said that there was no bride in the city, because she came from another place, and sat for a while in the gate, and she thought that no one knew that I had gone in to her. After this, we came into Egypt to Joseph, because of the famine. I was forty-six years old, and I lived there seventy-three years.

13. Greed, Pride, and Fornication

"Now, my children, in whatever things I command you, listen to your father, and keep all my sayings to perform the ordinances of the Lord, and to obey the command of the Lord God. Do not walk after your lusts, nor in the thoughts of your imaginations in the haughtiness of your heart. Do not glory in the works of the strength of youth, for this also is evil in the eyes of the Lord. For since I also gloried that in wars the face of no beautiful woman ever deceived me, and upbraided Reuben my brother concerning Bilhah, the wife of my father, the spirits of jealousy and of fornication arrayed themselves within me, until I sinned with Bathshua the Canaanite, and Tamar who was espoused to my sons. I said to my father-in-law, 'I will counsel with my father, and so will I take your daughter.' He showed me a boundless store of gold in his daughter's behalf, for he was a king. He decked her with gold and pearls, and caused her to pour out wine for us at the feast in womanly beauty. The wine led my eyes astray, and pleasure blinded my heart; and I loved her, and I fell, and transgressed the commandment of the Lord and the commandment of my fathers, and I married her. The Lord rewarded me according to the thought of my heart, insomuch that I had no joy in her children.

14. Deception of Alcohol

"My children, do not be drunk with wine; for wine turns the mind away from the truth, kindles the passion of lust, and leads the eyes into error. Fornication uses wine to create fantasies for the mind. These two take away man's power of self-control. If a man drinks to a state of drunkenness, his mind becomes filled with filthy thoughts of fornication, and if the woman is present, he sins without a second thought. Such is wine, my children. A drunkard respects no one. It also made me err, so that I was not ashamed of the multitude in the city, I turned aside unto Tamar in front of them all, and I sinned, and I uncovered the covering of the shame of my sons. After I was drunk with wine, I disobeyed God's commandment and took a Canaanite wife. Therefore, my children, whoever drinks wine lacks discretion. Here is discretion: drink only as long as you can be decent; if you go beyond this point, the wine deceives your mind and works evil. It makes the drunkard talk filthily, transgress, and not be ashamed. It even causes him to glory in his dishonor, believing he has done well.

15. Fornication Enslaves

"He who fornicates, and uncovers his nakedness, has become the servant of fornication, and cannot escape its power, as I also was uncovered. For I gave my staff, the symbol of my tribe; my girdle, the symbol of my power; and my crown, which is the glory of my kingdom. Then I repented of these things, and took no wine or flesh until my old age, nor did I behold any joy. An angel of God showed me that women eternally bear rule over kings and beggars alike. They take away the king's glory, and the valiant man's strength, and they take from the beggar even the little that keeps him from poverty.

16. Moderation

"Therefore, my children, observe moderation in wine; for it brings out four evils: lust, wrath, rioting, and greed. If you drink wine in gladness, with humility, and with the fear of God, you will live. If you do not drink with humility, and the fear of God leaves you, then comes drunkenness, and pride sets in. Even if you never drink, guard yourselves lest you sin in words of outrage, fighting, or slander, transgressing the commandments of God; or you will perish before your time. Moreover, drunkenness causes you to divulge the mysteries of God and men to unbelievers, just as I revealed the commandments of God and the mysteries of Jacob, my father, to the Canaanite, Bathshua, to whom God forbade to declare them. Wine is also a cause of war and confusion.

17. Judah's Charge

"I charge you, therefore, my children, not to love money, nor to gaze upon the beauty of women; because, for the sake of money and beauty, I was led astray to Bathshua the Canaanite. I know that because of these two things my descendants will fall into wickedness. Even wise men among my sons they will mar, and will cause the kingdom of Judah to be diminished, which the Lord gave me because of my obedience to my father. For I never disobeyed a word of Jacob my father; I did everything he commanded. Abraham, my great-grandfather, blessed me that I should be king in Israel, and Isaac further blessed me in like manner. I know that from me will the kingdom be established.

18. The Books of Enoch

"I have also read in the books of Enoch, the Righteous, [the books of Enoch and his fathers'] what evils you will do in the last days. Guard against fornication and the love of money. Listen to your father, for these things separate you from the law of God, blind the understanding of the soul, teach arrogance, and take away your compassion. They rob your soul of all goodness, bind you in troubles, take away your sleep, devour your flesh, and hinder the sacrifices of God. They cause you to forget the blessing, ignore the prophets, and trouble you with ungodliness. You cannot serve these two passions and obey the commandments of God, because they blind your soul, and make those who walk in the daytime like they were walking in the night.

19. Guard Against Your Weaknesses
"My children, the love of money leads to idolatry; because, when money leads men astray they talk about false gods, and it causes them to fall into madness. For the sake of money, I lost my children, and only through repentance, humbling my soul, and the prayers of Jacob my father, I found forgiveness. The God of my fathers, who is pitiful and merciful, pardoned me, because I did it in ignorance. The Prince of Deceit blinded me, and I was ignorant in my humanity, being corrupted in sins; and I learned of my own weakness while thinking myself unconquerable.

20. Truth or Error
"Learn therefore, my children, that two spirits wait upon man — the spirit of truth and the spirit of error. Among them stands the understanding of the mind. Truth and error are written on the hearts of men, and the Lord knows each one. There is no time that the works of men can be hidden from Him. Each man must decide deep within his own heart whether to be true or not. The Spirit of Truth testifies all things, and accuses all. He who sins is destroyed by his own heart, and cannot raise his face unto the Judge.

21. Obey Levi

"My children, love Levi, that you may live. Do not rebel against him, or you will be utterly destroyed. The Lord gave me the kingdom, and him the priesthood, and He set the kingdom beneath the priesthood. He gave me the things upon the earth; but to him, the heavenly things. As the heaven is higher than the earth, so is the priesthood of God higher than the kingdom upon the earth. The Lord chose him above you, to draw near to Him, and to eat of His table and first-fruits, even the choice things of the sons of Israel, and you will be to them as a sea. For as on the sea, just and unjust are tossed about. Some are taken into captivity while others are enriched, so also will every type of man be in you. Some are in jeopardy and taken captive, and others will grow rich by means of plunder. Those who rule will be as great sea-monsters, swallowing up men like fishes. They will enslave free sons and daughters. They will plunder houses, lands, flocks, and money. With the flesh of many they will wrongfully feed the ravens and the cranes; and they will go further in evil, advancing in greed. There will be false prophets like tempests, and they will persecute all righteous men.

22. Judah's Seed is King Forever

"The Lord will bring divisions on them, one against another, and there will be continual wars in Israel. Among men of another race will my kingdom be brought to an end, until the salvation of Israel will come, until the appearing of the God of Righteousness, that Jacob and all the Gentiles may rest in peace. He will guard the might of my kingdom forever: for the Lord swore to me with an

Testament of Judah

oath that the kingdom should never fail from me, and from my seed, for all days, even forever.

23. Sins of His Children

"I am much grieved, my children, because you will sin against the kingdom with lewdness, witchcraft, idolatry, and by seeking those who have familiar spirits. You will make your daughters singing girls and harlots for divinations and demons of error, and you will be mingled in Gentile pollution. For these things, the Lord will bring on you famine, pestilence, death by the sword, avenging siege, dogs for rending enemies to pieces, revilings of friends, destruction, blindness, children slaughtered, wives carried off, and possessions plundered. The temple of God will be in flames and your land desolated. You will be enslaved among the Gentiles, and they will make some of you eunuchs for their wives. Whenever you return to the Lord with humility of heart, repenting and walking in all the commandments of God, then will the Lord visit you in mercy and love, bringing you out of the bondage of your enemies.

24. The Messiah

"After these things will a star arise to you from Jacob in peace, and a man will rise from my seed, like the Sun of Righteousness, walking with the sons of men in meekness and righteousness, and no sin will be found in Him. The heavens will be opened above Him, to shed forth the blessing of the Spirit from the Holy Father. He will shed forth a spirit of grace on you. You will be to Him sons in truth, and you will walk in His commandments, the first and the last. This is the Branch of God Most High, and this is the well-spring unto life for all flesh. Then the scepter of my kingdom will shine forth, and from your root a stem will arise. In it will arise a rod of righteousness to the Gentiles, to judge and to save all that call upon the Lord.

25. The Resurrection

"After these things will Abraham, Isaac, and Jacob arise unto life. I and my brothers will be chiefs, even your scepter in Israel: Levi first, I the second, Joseph third, Benjamin fourth, Simeon fifth, Issachar sixth, and so all in order. The Lord blessed Levi with the Angel of the Presence; me with the powers of glory; Simeon with the heaven; Reuben with the earth; Issachar with the sea; Zebulun with the mountains; Joseph with the tabernacle; Benjamin with the lights of heaven; Dan with the fatness of earth; Naphtali with the sun; Gad with the olive; Asher... There will be one people of the Lord, and one tongue. There will no more be a spirit of deceit of Belial, for he will be cast into the fire forever. Those who have died in grief will rise in joy. Those who have lived in poverty for the Lord's sake will be made rich, and those who have been in want will be filled. Those who have been weak will be made strong, and those who have been put to death for the Lord's sake will awake in life. The hearts of Jacob will run in joyfulness, and the eagles of Israel will fly in gladness; but the ungodly will lament, and sinners all weep, and all the people will glorify the Lord forever.

26. Judah's Death

"My children, observe the whole law of the Lord, for there is hope for all those who follow His way correctly. Today I die, a hundred and nineteen years old. Let no one bury me in costly apparel, nor tear open my bowels, for this is what kings do. Carry me up to Hebron with you."

Judah, when he had said these things, fell asleep; and his sons did according to all that he commanded them, and they buried him in Hebron with his fathers.

Commentary

Judah 21 warns that false prophets will arise and persecute the righteous.

Judah 22 says the Messiah is from Judah's line and will bring salvation.

Judah 23 sees a vision of the temple of God in flames, and the nation of Israel desolated.

Judah 24 teaches that the Messiah is a star of Jacob, a branch, and a rod of the Gentiles. Compare this to Numbers 24:17.

Judah 25 teaches that there will be a future Resurrection.

Testament of Issachar

Concerning Simplicity

1. Issachar

The record of the words of Issachar. He called his sons, and said to them, "My children, listen to Issachar, your father; you who are beloved of the Lord. I was the fifth son born to Jacob, even the hire of the mandrakes.[gg] For Reuben brought in mandrakes from the field, and Rachel met him and took them. Reuben wept, and at his voice Leah, my mother, came out. These mandrakes were sweet-smelling apples which the land of Aram produced on high ground below a ravine of water. Rachel said, 'I will not give them to you. They will be for my children.' There were two apples; and Leah said, 'Isn't it enough that you have taken the husband of my virginity. Will you also take these?' Rachel said, 'I will give you Jacob for tonight and you give me your son's mandrakes.' Leah said to her, 'Don't boast or be prideful; for Jacob is mine, and I am the wife of his youth.' But Rachel said, 'How so? He was espoused to me first. He served our father fourteen years for me! It is not my fault that our father was a deceiver and that deception has increased upon the earth. If it was not for deception, you would have never seen the face of Jacob. You are not his wife, but a pawn our father used. He also deceived me, and sent me away

---

[gg] Genesis 30:14-18

that night. If I had been there, the deception would not have happened.' Rachel said, 'Take one mandrake, and for the other you will hire him from me for one night.' Jacob knew Leah, and she conceived and bare me, and on account of the hire I was called Issachar.

2. Rachel's Mandrakes
"Then an angel of the Lord appeared to Jacob, saying, 'Rachel will bear two children; for she has refused the company of her husband, and has chosen continency.' If my mother, Leah, had not given up the two apples for the sake of his company, she would have borne eight sons. Because of the mandrakes, the Lord visited Rachel and she bore two sons and Leah only bore six. God knew that for the sake of children she wished to company with Jacob, and not just for pleasure. For she went further, and on the morrow too gave up Jacob that she might receive also the other mandrake. Therefore, the Lord listened to Rachel because of the mandrakes; for though she desired them, she ate them not, but brought them to the priest of the Most High who was at that time,[hh] and offered them up in the house of the Lord.

3. Simplicity of life
"When I grew up, I walked in uprightness of heart, and I became a husbandman for my parents and my brothers. I brought in fruits from the field in their season. My father blessed me, for he saw that I walked in simplicity. I was

---

[hh] This was most likely Isaac. Shem, Eber, and Abraham were already dead.

not a busybody, malicious, nor slanderous. I never spoke against anyone, nor did I criticize anyone, but walked in simplicity. Therefore, when I was thirty years old I married, for my labor wore away my strength, and I was never a womanizer. I was content in my work and sleep, and my father always rejoiced in my simplicity. Out of my produce I offered first-fruits to the Lord by the hands of the priests[ii], then to my father, and then took for myself. The Lord increased His benefits twofold in my hands; and Jacob knew that God blessed my simplicity, for I helped the poor and distressed out of the good things of the earth in simplicity of heart.

4. The Righteousness of Simplicity

"Listen, my children. Walk in simplicity of heart, for it brings all that is well-pleasing to the Lord. The simple do not covet gold, defraud his neighbor, long after many dainties, delight in varied apparel, nor desire long life for himself.[jj] Instead, he waits for the will of God, and the spirits of error have no power against him. He does not allow his mind to be corrupted by lust, envy, jealousy, or greed. He walks in righteousness and sees everything in simplicity, not focusing on the malice from the errors of the world. He does not learn to pervert any of the commandments of the Lord.

[ii] The Melchizedekian priesthood (Shem and Eber) and the priesthood of Levi existed at this time. The Aaronic priesthood was not yet established.
[jj] Either thinking he has plenty of time to repent or seeking ungodly ways to extend his life.

5. Seek God's Blessing

"My children, keep God's law, live in simplicity, and walk without guile. Do not curiously pry into your neighbor's business. Instead, love the Lord and your neighbor. Have compassion on the poor and weak. Work hard and offer gifts unto the Lord with thanksgiving; for the Lord blessed me with the first-fruits of the earth, as He blessed all the saints from Abel even until now. The portion God gave you is the fatness of the earth, whose fruits are raised by toil; for our father Jacob blessed me with blessings of the earth and of first-fruits. The Lord glorified Levi and Judah among the sons of Jacob; for the Lord made choice of them. He gave the priesthood to one, and the kingdom to the other. Therefore, obey them, and walk in the simplicity of your father; for unto Gad has it been given to destroy the temptations that are coming upon Israel.

6. The End Times

"My children, I know that in the last times your sons will forsake simplicity. Their lives will be filled with greed and malice. They will forsake the commandments of the Lord, will cleave unto Belial. They will leave simplicity, follow wickedness, and will be dispersed among the Gentiles, serving their enemies. Teach your children what awaits them, so that if they sin, they may quickly return to the Lord; for He is merciful, and will deliver them even to bring them back into their land.

7. Issachar's Last Days

"I am a hundred and twenty-two years old, and I never committed a sin unto death. I have not known any woman except my wife. I never committed fornication, got drunk, or coveted anything that was my neighbor's. Guile never entered in my heart nor did a lie ever pass through my lips. If any man grieved, I wept with him, and I shared my bread with the poor. I never ate alone. I moved no landmark in all my days. I was godly and truthful. I loved the Lord with all my strength and every man like they were my own children. My children, if you do these things, every spirit of Belial will flee from you, malicious men will not rule over you, and you will subdue every wild beast. God will be with you. Walk among men in simplicity of heart."

Issachar commanded them that they should carry him up to Hebron, and bury him there in the cave with his fathers. He stretched out his feet and died, the fifth son of Jacob, in a good old age. With every limb sound, and with strength unabated, he slept the eternal sleep.

Commentary
Issachar 6 predicts a dispersion from the land.

Testament of Zebulun

Concerning Compassion and Mercy.

1. Zebulun

The record of Zebulun, which he instructed his children in the hundred and fourteenth year of his life, thirty-two years after the death of Joseph. He said to them, "Listen to me, my sons. I, Zebulun, am a good gift to my parents. For when I was born, our father had greatly increased in both flocks and herds, when with the streaked rods he had his portion. My children, I know throughout my life I sinned in my thoughts. I do not remember actually committing a sin, except the sin of ignorance which I committed against Joseph; for I helped my brothers and did not tell my father what had happened. I cried secretly, because I was afraid of my brothers. They had all agreed together, that if anyone should declare the secret, he should be slain with the sword. But when they wished to kill him, I pleaded with them to not be guilty of this iniquity.

2. Joseph Sold

"Simeon and Gad came against Joseph to kill him. Joseph fell upon his face, and said unto them, 'Pity me, my brothers, have compassion for the sake of Jacob our father. Do not kill me. I am innocent. I have not sinned against you. If I have sinned, then punish me, but do not kill me. Think of what it will do to Jacob, our father.'

When I heard him say those words, I pitied him and began to weep. My heart melted, and I became sick to my stomach. Joseph also wept, and I wept with him. My heart pounded, and I trembled. When Joseph saw them coming against him to kill him, he fled behind me, begging them. Reuben said, 'My brothers, let us not kill him, but let us cast him into one of these dry pits which our fathers dug.' The Lord kept those wells dry in order to preserve Joseph's life, because after he was sold to the Ishmaelites, water sprung up from them.

3. Law of Enoch
"I had no share in the money obtained for Joseph. But Simeon, Gad, and six of our brothers took the money, and bought sandals for themselves, their wives, and their children, saying, 'We will not eat of it, for it is the price of our brother's blood, but will tread it down under foot, because he said that he was king over us, and so let us see what his dreams mean.' It is written in the law of Enoch, that whosoever will not raise up seed to his brother, his sandal will be unloosed, and they will spit into his face. Joseph's brothers did not wish him to live, and the Lord loosed unto them the sandal of Joseph. For when they came into Egypt, they were unloosed by Joseph's servants before the gate, and so made subject to Joseph in the Egyptian way. Not only that, but they were spit upon also, falling down before him immediately, and so they were put to shame before the Egyptians. After this, the Egyptians heard all the evils which we had done to Joseph.

4. Joseph Sold

After these things, they brought forth food. For two days and nights I tasted nothing, through pity for Joseph. Judah did not eat with them, but watched the pit; for he was afraid that Simeon and Gad would go back and kill him. When they saw that I did not eat, they set me to watch him until he was sold. He remained in the pit three days and three nights, and so was sold starving. When Reuben heard that while he was away Joseph had been sold, he rent his clothes about him, and mourned, saying, 'How will I look in the face of Jacob, my father?' He took the money, and ran after the merchants, but could not find them; for they left the main road. Reuben did not eat that day. Dan came up to him, and said, 'Don't worry; I have figured out what to say to our father Jacob. Let us kill a kid of the goats, and dip in it the coat of Joseph; and we will say, "Look and see if this is your son's coat." For they stripped Joseph of the coat his father gave him and put slave's clothes on him before they sold him. Now Simeon had the coat, and would not give it up, wishing to rend it with his sword; for he was angry that Joseph lived, and that he had not killed him. We all rose up together against him, and said, 'If you do not give it up, we will say that you alone did this wickedness in Israel,' and so he gave it up, and they did as Dan had said.

5. Sin Causes Sickness

"Now, my children, I bid you to keep the commands of the Lord. Show mercy to your neighbor, and have compassion towards all, not just men, but also animals. For this thing's sake, the Lord blessed me. When all my brothers were sick, I escaped without sickness, for the Lord knows each person's heart. Therefore, have compassion, because whatever a man does to his neighbor, the Lord will do to him. The sons of my brothers were sick and dying because of Joseph, because they did not show mercy in their hearts; but my sons were preserved without sickness, as you know. When I was in Canaan, by the seacoast, I caught spoil of fish for Jacob, my father; and when many were drowned in the sea, I survived unhurt.

6. Sailing and Fishing

"I was the first who made a boat to sail upon the sea, for the Lord gave me understanding and wisdom therein. I let down a rudder behind it, and stretched a sail on an upright mast in the midst; and sailed along the shores. I caught fish for the house of my father until we went into Egypt. Through compassion, I gave of my fish to every stranger. If any man were a stranger, or sick, or aged, I boiled the fish and dressed them well, and offered them to all men as every man had need, bringing them together and having compassion upon them. Therefore, the Lord granted me to catch many fish; for he that imparts unto his neighbor, receives much more from the Lord. For five years I caught fish, and gave to every man whom I saw, and brought sufficient for all the house of my father. In the summer, I caught fish, and in the winter, I kept sheep with my brothers.

Testament of Zebulun

7. Showing Mercy

"Now I will declare unto you what I did. I saw a man in distress and nakedness in wintertime, and had compassion upon him. I secretly gave him a garment from my house. Do the same from which God has given to you. Impartially show compassion and mercy to all men, and give to every man with a good heart. If you have nothing to give at that time, at least show him mercy. When I had nothing to give, I walked with them, listened, and gave them advice.

8. Compassion and Mercy

"Show compassion to everyone with mercy, so the Lord will be compassionate and merciful to you. God will show compassion in the last days and will dwell with all those who practice mercy. If you have no compassion on your neighbor, God will have no compassion for you. When we went down into Egypt, Joseph bore no malice against us. When he saw me, he was filled with compassion. Take his example. Forsake malice, love one another, and plan no evil for your brother; for this breaks unity, divides families, and troubles the soul. Whoever bears malice cannot show mercy.

9. Two Kingdoms and Two Captivities

"Consider a river that can move trees and rocks. If it is divided into many small streams, the earth just dries them up. So will you be if you become divided. Do not divide yourselves into two heads, for everything which the Lord made has only one head. He gave pairs of shoulders, hands, and feet, but all the members are subject unto the one head. I have learned by the writing of my fathers, that in the last days you will depart from the Lord, and be divided in Israel. You will follow two kings, work every abomination, and worship every idol. Your enemies will lead you captive, and you will dwell among the nations with all infirmities, tribulations, and anguish of soul. After these things, you will remember the Lord, and repent. He will lead you back, for He is merciful and full of compassion, not imputing evil to the sons of men because they are flesh. The spirits of error deceive them in all their ways. After these things the Lord Himself will arise to you.[kk] The light of righteousness, healing, and compassion will be in His wings. He will redeem all captivity of the sons of men from Belial, and every spirit of error will be trodden down. He will bring back all the nations to zeal for Him, and you will see God in the fashion of a man whom the Lord will choose. Jerusalem is His name. With the wickedness of your words will you provoke Him to anger again, and you will be cast away, even unto the time of consummation.

10. Zebulun's Death

"My children, do not grieve over my death. I will arise once more in your midst, as a ruler in the midst of his sons. I will rejoice in the midst of my tribe, as many as have kept the law of the Lord, and the commandments of Zebulun their father. But the Lord will destroy the ungodly with everlasting fire throughout all generations. I

[kk] Mathew 4:14-16. Zebulon and Naphtali, the Galilee of the Gentiles.

Testament of Zebulun

am quickly going to my rest, as did my fathers. Fear the Lord your God with all your strength, all the days of your life."

When he had said these things, he fell calmly asleep, and his sons laid him in a coffin. Afterwards they carried him up to Hebron, and buried him with his fathers.

Commentary

Zebulun 3 states that the law of Enoch contains the Mosaic ritual of the brother-in-law.

Zebulun 9 teaches that Israel will split into two kingdoms. They will have two captivities (which were the Babylonian and Roman). The *Writings of the Fathers*, teach that the Messiah starts His ministry in the land of Zebulun, and that the Messiah is both God and man.

Zebulun 10 teaches that there will be a Resurrection.

Testament of Dan

Concerning Anger and Lying

1. Dan's Hatred

The record of the words of Dan, which he spoke to his sons in his last days. In the hundred and twenty-fifth year of his life he called together his family, and said, "Listen to my words, sons of Dan. I know in my heart, that throughout my whole life, God has been pleased with truth and just dealing. Lying and anger are evil; because they teach man all kinds of wickedness. My children, I confess that in my heart I rejoiced concerning the death of Joseph, a true and good man. I rejoiced at the selling of Joseph, because our father loved him more than us. I became jealous and vain because I was his son, too. A satanic spirit caused me to hate Joseph so much I wanted to kill him with a sword. With Joseph gone, my father would love me in the way he did him. This spirit of anger so consumed me that I thought of nothing else but to kill him. But the God of Jacob, our father, kept him from me. I never found him alone. I thank God for not allowing it or there would be two less tribes in Israel.

2. Hatred and Envy

"My children, I am dying, and I tell you the truth: unless you avoid lying and anger, and embrace love, truth, and patience, you will perish. There is blindness in anger, my children, and no angry man trusts anyone to tell the truth.

Testament of Dan

He treats his father and mother as enemies, and his brother like he does not know him. Even if his brother is a prophet of the Lord, he disobeys him. He will not regard a righteous man, and he ignores his friends. Anger surrounds him with nets of deceit, blinds his natural eyes, and darkens his mind through lies. He sees what he wants to see. He only sees his own hatred, all because of envy.

3. Wrath of the Rich and Poor

"My children, anger tricks you. It takes over your body and masters your soul. It uses you to do all manner of sin. Your mind justifies what you have done because you refuse to see it as sin. A rich man's anger is threefold: it comes through his servants, his influence in the courts, and his direct anger. A poor man's anger is twofold: his direct anger, and his manipulation and lies behind the scenes. Through both, Satan works through cruelty and lying.

4. How to Avoid Being Attacked with Anger

"Understand the vanity of anger. At first, it only attacks by words. If agitated, it attacks with deeds which then afflict the mind and create bitterness. Therefore, when anyone speaks against you, do not show anger. If any man praises you, do not show pride. If you do, it may stir up another's anger against you. It will only cause you trouble. If you fall into some loss, remember God is in control and your anger about it will only lead to bitterness, making everything much worse. Bitterness always leads to two things: anger and lying. They work hand in hand, causing the Lord to depart and Belial to rule over you.

5. Last Days Prophecy

"My children, observe the commandments of the Lord, and keep His law. Depart from anger, hate, and lying, and the Lord will dwell with you, and Belial will flee from you. Speak truth to each other, and you will not fall into lust and confusion. Instead, you will have the peace of God, and no war will prevail over you. Love the Lord and each other with a true heart all your life. For I know that in the last days you will depart from the Lord, and will provoke Levi unto anger, and will fight against Judah; but you will not prevail against them. An angel of the Lord will guide them both and by them Israel will stand. When you depart from the Lord, you will walk in all kinds of evil, working the abominations of the Gentiles and going astray with ungodly women. The spirits of error will work in you with all malice. I have read in the book of Enoch the Righteous that your prince is Satan. All the spirits of fornication and pride will be subject unto Levi, but they will lay a snare for the sons of Levi to cause them to sin before the Lord. My sons will draw near unto Levi and sin with them in all things. The sons of Judah will be covetous, plundering other men's goods like lions. Therefore, you will be led away with them into captivity, and there you will receive all the plagues of Egypt, and all the malice of the Gentiles. When you return to the Lord, you will obtain mercy, and He will bring you into His sanctuary, calling peace upon you. There will rise unto you from the tribes of Judah and of Levi the salvation of

Testament of Dan

the Lord. He will make war against Belial, and He will give the vengeance of victory to our coasts. He will take the captivity from Belial, even the souls of the saints, and will turn disobedient hearts unto the Lord. He will give everlasting peace to those who call upon Him. The saints will rest in Eden, and the righteous will rejoice in the New Jerusalem, which will be to the glory of God forever and ever. No longer will Jerusalem endure desolation, nor Israel be led captive. The Lord will be in the midst of her, dwelling among men, even the Holy One of Israel reigning over them in humility and in poverty. He who believes on Him will reign in truth in the heavens.

6. The Savior

"My children, fear the Lord, and guard against Satan and his spirits. Draw close to God, and to the Angel that intercedes for you, for He is a mediator between God and man[ll] for the peace of Israel. He will stand up against the kingdom of the enemy. Therefore, the enemy is eager to destroy all that call upon the Lord. For he knows that in the day Israel believes, the kingdom of the enemy will be destroyed. The very angel of peace will strengthen Israel, so that it will not fall into extreme evil. It will be in the time of the iniquity of Israel, that the Lord will depart from them, and will go after those who do His will, for unto none of His angels will it be as unto him. His name in every place of Israel, and among the Gentiles will be Savior.[mm] Therefore, keep from every evil work, anger,

---

[ll] 1 Timothy 2:5
[mm] Yeshua

and all lying. Love truth and patience. Teach your children everything I told you so that the Father of the Gentiles may receive you. He is true and patient, meek and lowly, and teaches by His works the law of God. Depart from unrighteousness, and hold on to the righteousness of the law of the Lord. Bury me near my fathers."

7. Dan's Death
When he had said these things, he kissed them, and slept the long sleep. His sons buried him in Egypt, and later they carried up his bones to the side of Abraham, Isaac, and Jacob. Nevertheless, as Dan had prophesied to them that they should forget the law of their God, and should be alienated from the land of their inheritance, and from the race of Israel, and from their kindred, so also it came to pass.

Commentary
Dan 5 states that there will be a rebellion against Levi and Judah. Enoch wrote that Satan becomes the prince over the rebels. Eventually there will be a New Jerusalem in the eternal age.

Dan 6 predicts the great diaspora and the church age. Eventually Israel will accept the Messiah. Dan calls God the *Father of the Gentiles*.

Testament of Naphtali

Concerning Natural Goodness

1. Naphtali

The record of the testament of Naphtali, what things he ordained at the time of his death in the hundred and thirty-second year of his life. When his sons were gathered together in the seventh month, the fourth day of the month, while he was still in good health, he made them a feast. After he awoke the next morning, he said to them, "I am dying," but they did not believe him. He blessed the Lord, and affirmed that after the previous day's feast he would die. He began then to say to his sons, "Listen, my children. I was born from Bilhah. Because Rachel dealt craftily, and gave Bilhah in place of herself to Jacob, she bore me upon Rachel's lap. Therefore, I was called Naphtali. Rachel loved me because I was born upon her lap. When I was of young and tender form, she was used to kiss me, and say, 'I hope I have a son just like you!' Joseph turned out just like me in many ways, just as Rachel prayed. <u>Now my mother was Bilhah, daughter of Rotheus, the brother of Deborah, Rebecca's nurse, and she was born on the same day with Rachel. Rotheus was of the family of Abraham, a Chaldean, God-fearing, free-born and noble. He was taken captive, and bought by Laban, who gave him Aena his handmaid for a wife. She bore a daughter, and called her Zilpah, after the name of the village in which he had been taken captive. Next, she</u>

bore Bilhah, saying, "My daughter is eager after what is new," for immediately after she was born she was eager for the breast.[nn]

2. Find Your Calling

"Since I was swift on my feet like a deer, my father Jacob appointed me for all errands and messages, and as a deer he gave me his blessing[oo]. As the potter creates clay vessels designed for different purposes, so the Lord designs a body for the unique spirit it is to contain. Differences from one body to another are by design, not chance. As the potter knows what each vessel can and cannot do, so the Lord knows each person. He knows how much good and evil they are capable of, and when they can turn evil. God knows everything about every one of His creations and man is created in His image. Man's work depends on his strength, his mind, his purpose, what he practices, and what is in his heart. This can be known by observing his speech, desires, dreams, his soul, and his patterns of life. By observing these, you can know if he belongs to the Lord or Belial. You can see and hear the division between light and darkness in men and women. No group or race is superior to another. Everyone has five senses, minds, and hearts with all the same emotions. My children, practice righteousness in the fear of God, and do nothing out of its proper order. Remember an eye cannot hear, neither can darkness do the works of light.

[nn] 4Q215 Fragment 1
[oo] Genesis 49:21

3. Do not Change God's Word

"Do not corrupt yourselves by excess, or deceive yourselves with empty words.[pp] If your mouth is silent and your heart is pure, you will be able follow the will of God, and resist the will of the devil. The sun, moon, and stars do not change their order. Do not try to change the law of God into what you want it to be. Nations went astray, deserted the Lord, changed their order, and worshipped stones and wood, following spirits of error. Do not be like them, my children. Recognize that the Lord created all things, and only He is to be worshipped. Do not become like Sodom, who changed the order of their nature, in the same manner as the Watchers changed the order of their nature. They are the cause of the Flood and the desolation of the earth.

4. Prophecy

"These things I say, my children, for I have read in the holy writing of Enoch that you also will depart from the Lord, walking in the wickedness of the Gentiles, and the iniquity of Sodom. The Lord will bring captivity upon you. There you will serve your enemies, and you will be covered with all affliction and tribulation, until the Lord has consumed you all. After that, when you are few, you will return and acknowledge the Lord your God. He will bring you back into your own land, according to His abundant mercy. After you return to the land of your fathers, you will again forget the Lord and deal wickedly.

[pp] Ephesians 5:6

The Lord will scatter you upon the face of all the earth until the compassion of the Lord will come, a Man working righteousness and showing mercy unto all who are afar off, and who are near.

5. Vision of the Sun and Moon

"In the fortieth year of my life, I saw in a vision the sun and the moon standing still on the Mount of Olives, at the east of Jerusalem. Isaac, my grandfather, said to us, 'Run and lay hold of them, each one according to his strength; and he that seizes them, his will be the sun and the moon.' Then we all ran together, and Levi laid hold of the sun, and Judah outran the others and seized the moon, and they were both lifted up with them.^{qq} When Levi became as a sun, a certain young man gave to him twelve palm branches. Judah was bright as the moon, and under his feet were twelve rays. Levi and Judah ran, and laid hold of one another. There was a bull on the earth, having two great horns, and an eagle's wings upon his back. We wanted to seize him, but could not. Joseph outran us, and took him, and ascended on high with him. I saw, for I was there, and behold, a holy writing appeared to us. It had written on it: Assyrians, Medes, Persians, [Elamites, Gelachæans,] Chaldeans, Syrians, will possess in captivity the twelve tribes of Israel.^{rr}

[Aramaic Version adds this to the end of chapter 5.]

---

^{qq} Aramaic adds "we each caught a star except for Joseph."
^{rr} "Elamites and Gelachaeans" are not in some manuscripts.

Joseph stretched out his staff and hit Judah, his brother. Judah said, 'Brother, why are you hitting me?' Joseph said, 'Because you have in your hand twelve staves [rays]. I have only one. Give me ten and there will be peace.' Judah refused. Joseph then beat him and took ten staves by force. Only two were left with Judah. Joseph then said to his ten brothers, 'Why follow Judah and Levi? Follow after me.' His brothers immediately left Levi and Judah and all that was left was Judah, Levi, and Benjamin. When Levi saw this, he descended from the sun saddened. Joseph said to Benjamin, his brother, 'Benjamin, you are also my bother. Come with me.' But Benjamin refused. That night a storm arose and separated Joseph from his brothers, so that no two were left together.

6. Second Dream

"After seven months, I saw our father, Jacob, standing by the Sea of Jamnia, and we, his sons, were with him. Then there came a ship sailing by, [full of dried flesh[ss]], without sailors or pilot. There was written upon the ship the name of Jacob. Our father said to us, 'Let us board our ship.' When we had gone on board, there arose a fierce storm, and a strong wind. Our father, who was holding the helm, flew away from us. We, being tossed with the wind, were carried over the sea. The ship was filled with water and beaten about with a mighty wave, so that it was nearly broken in pieces. Joseph fled away upon a little boat. We

---

[ss] "Full of dried flesh" is not in some manuscripts.

all were divided on twelve boards, and Levi and Judah were together. We were all scattered far away. Then Levi, clothed with sackcloth, prayed for us all unto the Lord. When the storm ceased, immediately the ship reached the land, as though in peace. Then Jacob our father came, and we all rejoiced together.

7. Jacob's Interpretation
"I told my father these two dreams. He said to me, 'These things must be fulfilled in their season, after Israel has endured many things.' Then my father said to me, 'I believe that Joseph is alive, for I see that the Lord always numbers him with you.' Then, weeping, he said, 'You live, Joseph, my child, but I cannot behold you, and you cannot see Jacob, your father.' We all wept when he said these things. My heart broke, wanting to tell him that Joseph had been sold, but I feared my brothers.

8. Proper Order
"My children, I have shown to you the last times, and all that will come to pass in Israel. Charge your children to be united with Levi and Judah. For through Judah will salvation arise to Israel, and Jacob will be blessed through him. For through his tribe God will be seen dwelling among men on the earth, to save the race of Israel. He will gather together the righteous from the Gentiles. If you work what is good, my children, both men and angels will bless you. God will be glorified through you among the Gentiles, and the devil will flee from you. The wild beasts will fear you, and the angels will cling to you. If a man raises a child well, he is kindly remembered. So God

remembers those who do good. Whoever does evil is cursed by man and angels, and God is dishonored among the heathen through him. The devil makes him his own peculiar instrument. Every wild beast will master him, and the Lord will hate him.

"The commandments of the law are twofold, and must be fulfilled through prudence. For instance, there is a season for a man to embrace his wife, and a season to abstain from her for prayer. So then, there are two commandments, and unless they be done in the proper order, they bring about sin. It is the same with the other commandments. Pursue godly wisdom, prudence, the understanding of the order of the commandments, and the laws of every work, that the Lord may love you."

9. Naphtali's Death

After he charged them with these words, he exhorted them that they should bury him in Hebron, with his fathers. When he ate and drank with a merry heart, he covered his face and died. His sons obeyed everything that Naphtali, their father, had commanded.

4Q215 (often referred to as the *Time of Righteousness*)

Fragment 1

"They will be hunted, afflicted, and oppressed by the trial of the pit but the elect of righteousness will forgive all

Ancient Testaments of the Patriarchs

their iniquity because of His mercy and His pious ones will refine them.^{tt} When the age of wickedness is complete, all unrighteousness will pass away. The time of righteousness is coming, and the earth will be full of the knowledge and glory of God. In this age of peace, the true laws and the righteous testimony will instruct those in the ways of God and in His mighty deeds forever. Every tongue will bless Him. Everyone will bow down to serve Him with one mind.^{uu} For He knew their deeds before they were created and divided their borders for the work of righteousness in their generations. For the dominion of righteousness is coming and He will raise up the throne of the ... and very high. Insight, prudence, and sound wisdom are proved by His holy design.^{vv}

Fragment 2

"...His holiness. He established them for ...
...He created them to renew...
...from his/its days, the darkness...
...for his appointed time ... darkness...
...for appointed times before ...
...host...

Fragment 3

"...To destroy earth in His anger and to renew it...
...Source of their knowledge because ..."

---

^{tt} Daniel 11:35
^{uu} Philippians 2:10-11; Isaiah 45:23-24; Every knee will bow and every tongue confess that Jesus is LORD.
^{vv} Luke 7:35; Wisdom is vindicated by her children.

Testament of Naphtali

Commentary

Naphtali 4 states that Enoch predicted the tribe of Naphtali would be drawn to the sin of Sodom, which in chapter 3 is related to the sin of the Watchers. There will be two expulsions.

Naphtali 5 reveals a prophecy very similar to one given by the prophet Gad.[ww] The sun is depicted as God's priesthood on earth, governed by Levi, and the moon is depicted as God's kingdom on earth, led by Judah. Israel would be oppressed by seven kingdoms: Assyrians, Medes, Persians, Chaldeans [Babylonians], Syrians and two others. See the prophecy outline for details.

Naphtali 8 teaches the Savior will come from the linage of Judah and will be both God and man. Righteous Gentiles will flock to Him.

In 4Q215 fragment 1, Naphtali says in the age of peace the Messiah will teach "the true laws of God," implying that the Levites perverted the laws of God and rejected the Messiah.

[ww] See *Ancient Book of Gad the Seer 1-2*.

Testament of Gad

Concerning Hatred

1. Gad
The record of the testament of Gad, and what things he spoke to his sons, in the hundred and twenty-seventh year of his life, saying: "I was the seventh son born to Jacob, and I was valiant in keeping the flocks. I guarded the flock at night. Whenever any wild beast came against the fold, I pursued and killed it. Joseph had been feeding the flock with us for about thirty days, but he was young and could not stand the heat. He got sick. He returned to Hebron to his father, who made him lie down, because he loved him. Joseph told our father that the sons of Zilpah and Bilhah were slaying the best of the beasts, and devouring them without the knowledge of Judah and Reuben. He had seen that I delivered a lamb out of the mouth of the bear, and I put the bear to death. I killed the lamb, because I did not think it would live, and we ate it. He told our father. I was angry with Joseph for that until the day that he was sold into Egypt. The spirit of hatred was in me, and I did not want to see or even hear Joseph. He rebuked us to our faces for having eaten of the flock without Judah. Whatever he told our father, he believed him.

2. The Sin of Hatred
"My children, I confess now my sin, that I often wished to kill him, because I hated him, and felt no mercy towards him. I hated his dreams even more. If I had the chance, I would have killed him. Therefore, Judah and I sold him to the Ishmaelites for thirty pieces of gold[xx]. We hid ten and showed the twenty to the brothers. I was bent on his destruction but my greed saved him. The God of my fathers delivered him from my hands, so I could not work iniquity in Israel.

3. Avoid Hatred at all Costs
"My children, listen to the words of truth. Walk in righteousness, and all the law of the Most High. Do not be led astray by hatred, for it causes all kinds of evil. The person who hates cannot see any righteousness in the person he hates. He only sees his hatred, evidenced by his slander and arrogance toward him. It blinds his soul. This happened to me because of my hatred toward Joseph.

4. Hatred and Envy
"My children, fear hatred. It works iniquity against the Lord Himself. It will not listen to His command to love his neighbor. It sins against God. If a brother stumbles, he is immediately slandered to all men, and rushed to judgment to be punished and slain. If he is a servant, his master accuses him severely and, if possible, kills him. Hatred worsens through envy. Just as love would pardon

---

[xx] Twenty pieces of silver; Genesis 37:28.

those condemned to die, hatred would slay the living, even those with a minor offence. Satan uses hatred along with impulsiveness to kill; but the spirit of love works with the law of God in patience, producing salvation.

5. Overcoming Hatred

"Hatred is evil, because it is always found with lying, dishonesty, and exaggeration. It brings darkness rather than light, calls the sweet bitter, and teaches slander, war, and violence. It fills the heart with the deadly poison of every evil. I say this to you from experience. Flee hatred, and cling to the love of the Lord. Righteousness casts out hatred. Humility destroys hatred. He who is just and humble is ashamed to do wrong, being reproved not by another, but by his own heart, because the Lord views his intent. He does not speak against any man, because the fear of the Most High overcomes hatred. Fearing to offend the Lord, he will not do any wrong to anyone, not even in thought. These things I finally learned, after I repented concerning Joseph. For true godly repentance destroys unbelief, drives away the darkness, enlightens, gives knowledge to the soul, and guides you to salvation. Those things you cannot learn from man, you learn through repentance. God punished me with a disease of the heart. If Jacob, my father, had not prayed for me I surly would have died. The sins of a man are the same things that destroy him. Just as I showed no mercy toward Joseph for eleven months, I suffered mercilessly just as long.

6. The Power of Forgiveness

"My children, put away hatred. Love one another in thought, word, and deed. I spoke kindly of Joseph when I was with my father, but privately hatred darkened my mind to the point I wanted to kill him. Love each other. And if a man sin against you, talk to him gently. Do not foster the poison of hatred or guile. If he confesses and repents, forgive him. If he denies it, do not argue with him, in case he swears, and you sin twice. Do not rebuke him publicly because it may cause others to hate you, or gossip about you, causing great sin. If he denies it but is convicted in his heart, do not speak of it any further. For he who denies but repents will do you no more harm. Instead, he will honor, respect, and be at peace with you. If he continues in his wrongdoing, forgive him from the heart, and give the vengeance to God.

7. Envy

"If a man prospers more than you, do not envy, but pray that he increases even more. This attitude will benefit you greatly. If he is further exalted, do not envy him but remember that we all die. Instead, praise God for what He has done. Focus on the things of the Lord, and your mind will rest and be at peace. If a man becomes rich by dishonesty, like Esau, do not be jealous, but wait on the Lord. The Lord will take his riches away or punish him if he does not repent. If he continues in sin, he will suffer eternal punishment. The poor who are free from envy, and thank the Lord for all things, are truly rich among men, because jealousy does not control them. Therefore, put away hatred, and love one another with a pure heart.

8. Gad's Death

"Teach your children these things, so that they honor Judah and Levi, for from them will the Lord raise up a Saviour to Israel. I know that eventually your children will depart from them, and walk in wickedness, mischief, and corruption before the Lord."

When he had rested for a little while, he told them, "My children, obey your father, and bury me near my fathers." Then he fell asleep in peace. After five years, they carried him up, and laid him in Hebron with his fathers.

Commentary

Gad 8 reveals that the Savior will come from the tribe of Judah.

Testament of Asher

Concerning Hypocrisy in Vice and Virtue

1. Asher

The record of the testament of Asher, what things he spoke to his sons in the hundred and twentieth year of his life. While he was still in health, he said to them: "My children, listen to me, I want to tell you what is right in the sight of God. God has given two ways to the sons of men, two different mindsets, or lifestyles, and they lead to two different eternities. The two ways are good and evil; and we each have two natures. Therefore, if the soul takes pleasure in good, all his actions are righteous. If he sins, he immediately repents, because his mind is focused on righteousness, he rejects evil, and this uproots the sin. If the soul focuses on evil, his actions begin to be evil. He drives away the good, and becomes increasingly evil. Belial rules over him and even the good he does perverts to evil because the poison is in his heart.

2. Evil that appears to be godly[yy]

"There are those who speak good for the sake of the evil, which only brings trouble.

[yy] 2 Timothy 3:5

Ancient Testaments of the Patriarchs

1. A man who shows no compassion upon a truly repentant sinner. This looks like righteousness, but is actually sin.

2. A man who chooses to live with, or even die for, an evil person because he loves him. This has an appearance of righteousness, but is actually sin.

3. There is a compassion that conceals evil in the name of mercy. It may seem good, but it only brings more evil. That kind compassion turns mercy into sin.

4. One person steals, cons, plunders, and defrauds, but pities the poor. He seems both good and evil, but in reality, he is only evil. When he defrauds his neighbor, he provokes God, and swears falsely against the Most High. Even though he pities and refreshes the poor, he sets aside the law of God defiling his soul. He may appear to be good, but in reality, he kills many and pities few.

5. Another person commits adultery and fornication, but abstains from meats. His fasting only works evil, and he perverts many through his power and wealth. The fornication turns his fasting into sin.

Testament of Asher

"Such men are like swine or hares[zz]; only half clean, but in truth they are unclean, God's heavenly tablets have declared.

3. The Hypocrite
"My children, do not be like the hypocrite, practicing both good and wickedness. Instead, hold fast only to what is good, for God rests in goodness and all men desire it. Flee wickedness. Destroy the devil by your good works. The hypocrites do not serve God, but their own lusts, pleasing Belial and other men like themselves.

4. Godliness that Appears to be Evil
"Hypocrites consider godly, single-minded men to be in error.

1. They say putting a murderer to death is evil, but in reality, it is a good work, because it uproots and destroys evil from the land.

2. They do not understand that it is not hypocritical to show mercy on a truly repentant adulterer and thief, but punish the unrepentant sinner, both are acts of righteousness because he follows the Lord's example, in that he refuses evil that appears to be good, and that which is obviously evil.

[zz] Leviticus 11:6-8

3. They also think it hypocritical to strive against those who carouse, but the righteous know that by tolerating sinners, they will pollute their souls and defile their own speech. It is a righteous act to both refrain from these actions and forcibly stop others from doing them. Such men are like stags and hinds, because in a wild condition they seem to be unclean, but they are altogether clean. They walk in a zeal for God, and abstain from what God also hates and forbids by His commandments, and they ward off the evil from the good.

5. The Single-minded

"My children, you see how that there are two sides to all things. One opposes the other, and one is hidden by the other. Death succeeds to life, dishonor to glory, night to day, and darkness to light; and all things are under the day, and just things under life. Everlasting life also awaits death. Nor may it be said that truth is a lie, nor right, wrong; for all truth is under the light, even as all things are under God. All these things I proved in my life, and I wandered not from the truth of the Lord. I searched out the commandments of the Most High, walking single-mindedly with all my strength unto that which is good.

6. Live a Righteous Life

"My children, remember the commandments of the Lord. Single-mindedly follow the truth, for the hypocrites receive twofold punishment. Hate the spirits of error that strive against men. Keep the law of the Lord, and do not practice evil with good. Practice only good, and keep all

Testament of Asher

of the commandments of the Lord. Conduct your lives by Him and rest in Him. Your actions will show if you are righteousness and whom you follow: the angels of God or the angels of Satan. If the soul dies troubled, it is because it was tormented by the evil spirits it served through its lusts and evil works. If the soul dies quietly and with joy, it is because God's peace has comforted him in life.

7. Recognize the Messiah

"My children, do not become as Sodom who perished forever because they did not recognize the angels of the Lord. I know that you will sin, and you will be delivered into the hands of your enemies. Your land will be made desolate, and you will be scattered unto the four corners of the earth. You will be disregarded in the Dispersion as useless water, until the Most High will visit the earth. He will come as man, eating and drinking with men, and in peace He will break the head of the dragon through water. He will save Israel and all nations, God speaking in the person of man. Therefore, teach these things to your children, so they will not disobey Him; for I have read in the heavenly tablets that you truly will disobey Him, and act ungodly against Him, not giving heed to the law of God, but to the commandments of men. Therefore, you will be scattered as Gad and Dan, my brothers, who will not know their own lands, tribe, or tongue; but the Lord will gather you together in faith through the hope of His tender mercy, for the sake of Abraham, Isaac, and Jacob."

8. Asher's Death

When he had said these things to them, he charged them, saying: "Bury me in Hebron." Then he fell into a peaceful sleep, and died. After this his sons did as he had charged them, and they carried him up and buried him with his fathers.

Commentary

Asher 7 predicts an expulsion to all nations. The Messiah is God incarnate appearing on earth, who will bring salvation for Israel and the Gentiles.

Testament of Joseph

Concerning Sobriety

1. Joseph

The record of the testament of Joseph: when he was about to die, he called his sons and his brothers together, and said to them: "My children and brothers, listen to Joseph, the beloved of Israel, your father. I have seen in my life envy and death, and I have not wandered in the truth of the Lord. My brothers hated me; but the Lord loved me. They wished me dead; but the God of my fathers guarded me. They threw me into a pit; but the Most High brought me back up. I was sold for a slave; but the Lord set me free. I was taken into captivity; but His strong hand comforted me. When I was hungry, the Lord Himself nourished me. When I was sick and alone, God was with me. When I was in prison, the Savior showed me favor and released me. Amid slanders, He rescued me and exalted me above all envy and guile.

2. Joseph's Trials

"Potiphar, the chief cook[aaa] of Pharaoh, entrusted to me his house, and I struggled against a shameless woman urging me to transgress with her; but the God of Israel, my father, guarded me from the burning flame. I was cast into prison, beaten, and mocked; but the Lord granted me

---

[aaa] Genesis 39:1 LXX and Josephus Ant. 2.4.1

to find pity in the sight of the keeper of the prison; for He will, in no wise, forsake those who fear Him, neither in darkness, nor bonds, nor tribulations, nor in necessities. For God is not a man. He cannot be ashamed, afraid, weak, or thrust aside. In every situation, He is there to comfort. He only departs for a little while to try your soul. In ten temptations He showed me approved, and in all of them I endured; for endurance is a mighty charm, and patience gives many good things.

3. Joseph and the Egyptian Woman

"How often did the Egyptian threaten me with death! How often did she give me over to punishment, and then call me back, and threaten me when I would not company with her! She said to me, 'You will be lord of me, and all that is mine, if you will give yourself unto me, and you will be as our master.' Therefore, I remembered the words of the fathers of my father Jacob, and I entered into my chamber and prayed unto the Lord; and I fasted in those seven years, and I appeared to my master as one living delicately, for they that fast for God's sake receive beauty of face. If one gave me wine, I drank it not. I fasted for three days, and took my food and gave it to the poor and sick. I sought the Lord early, and wept for the Egyptian woman of Memphis, for she troubled me unceasingly, and at night she came to me under the pretense of visiting me. At first, because she had no male child, she feigned to count me as a son. I prayed unto the Lord, and she bare a male child. Therefore, for a time she embraced me as a son, and I knew it not. Last of all, she sought to draw me into fornication. When I perceived it, I sorrowed even unto death. When she had gone out I came to myself, and I lamented for her many days, because I saw her guile and deceit. I declared unto her the words of the Most High, if perhaps she would turn from her evil lust.

4. Egyptian Woman's False Conversion
"How often she fawned upon me with words as a holy man, with guile in her talk, praising my chastity before her husband, while desiring to destroy me when we were alone. She lauded me openly as chaste, and in secret she said unto me, 'Do not be afraid of my husband; for he is convinced you are chaste, so that even should one tell him concerning us, he would never believe him.' For all these things, I lay upon the ground in sackcloth, and I besought God that the Lord would deliver me from the Egyptian. When she prevailed nothing, she came again to me under the plea of instruction, that she might know the word of the Lord. She said unto me, 'If you want me to abandon my idols, just tell me, and I will persuade my husband to depart from his idols, and we will walk in the law of your Lord.' I said unto her, 'The Lord does not want those who reverence Him to live in uncleanness, nor does He take pleasure in those who commit adultery.' She held her peace, longing to accomplish her evil desire. I gave myself yet more to fasting and prayer, that the Lord should deliver me from her.

5. The Threat of Murder
"At another time she said unto me, 'If you will not commit adultery, I will kill my husband, and so can I lawfully take you to be my husband.' When I heard this,

rent my garment, and said, 'Woman, reverence the Lord, and do not this evil deed, lest you be utterly destroyed; for I will declare your ungodly thought unto all men.' She therefore, being afraid, begged me not to tell her wickedness to anyone. She departed, soothing me with gifts, and sending to me every delight of the sons of men.

6. Egyptian Woman Tries Drugs

"She sent me food sprinkled with enchantments. When the eunuch who brought it came, I looked up and beheld a terrible man giving me with the dish, a sword, and I perceived that her scheme was for the deception of my soul. When he had gone out I wept, nor did I eat any of her food. After one day she came to me and observed the food, and said unto me, 'What is this? Why have you not eaten the food?' I said unto her, 'It is because you filled it with death. How said you, "I come not near to idols but to the Lord alone"? Now therefore know that the God of my father has revealed your wickedness to me by an angel, and I have kept it to convict you, if perhaps you may see it and repent. But that you may learn that the wickedness of the ungodly has no power over those who reverence God in chastity,' I took it and ate it before her, saying, 'The God of my fathers and the angel of Abraham will be with me.' She fell upon her face at my feet, and wept; and I raised her up and admonished her, and she promised to not to do this iniquity again.

7. The Threat of Suicide

"But because her heart was set upon me to commit lewdness, she sighed, and her countenance fell. When her husband saw her, he said unto her, 'Why is your countenance fallen?' She said, 'I have a heartache, and my spirit is grieved.' So, he comforted her. Then she rushed in to me while her husband was right outside, and said unto me, 'I will hang myself, or cast myself into a well or over a cliff, if you will not consent to me.' When I saw the spirit of Belial was troubling her, I prayed unto the Lord, and said unto her, 'Why are you troubled, disturbed, and blinded in sins? Remember that if you kill yourself, Sethon, your husband's concubine, your rival, will beat your children, and will erase all memory of you.' She said unto me, 'Then you do love me; this alone is sufficient for me, that you care for my life and my children. I have expectation that I will enjoy my desire.' She did not realize that it was because of my God I said this, not because of her. If anyone falls into the passion of a wicked desire, they become enslaved by it. She was so enslaved by her desire that she mistook any kind word from me as a sign that her wicked desire might soon be fulfilled.

8. Prison is the Answer to Joseph's Prayer

"I declare unto you, my children, that it was about the sixth hour when she departed from me; and I knelt before the Lord all that day, and continued all the night. About dawn I rose up weeping, and praying for a release from the Egyptian. At last, then, she laid hold of my garments, forcibly dragging me to have an affair with her. When, therefore, I saw that in her madness she was forcibly holding my garments, I fled away naked. She falsely accused me to her husband, and the Egyptian cast me into the prison in his house. The next day, he had me scourged and sent to the prison house. When, therefore, I was in fetters, the Egyptian woman fell sick from her vexation. I sang praises unto the Lord while I was in the abode of darkness, and with glad voice rejoiced and glorified my God only because by a pretext I had been rid of the Egyptian woman.

9. Wicked Woman Visits Joseph in Prison
"How often she had sent unto me, saying, 'Consent to fulfil my desire, and I will release you from your bonds, and free you from the darkness of the prison!' Not even in thoughts did I incline unto her. For God loves those who in a den of darkness fast with chastity, rather than those who in secret chambers live delicately without restraint. Whosoever lives in chastity, and desires also glory, and if the Most High knows that it is expedient for him, He bestows this also upon him, even as upon me. How often, though when she was sick, did she come down to me at odd times, and listened to my voice as I prayed! When I heard her groanings, I held my peace. For when I was in her house she used to bare her arms, breasts, and legs, so I might fall before her; for she was very beautiful, splendidly adorned for my deception. The Lord guarded me from her devices.

10. Patience, Fasting, and Prayer
"You see, my children, how great things come through patience with prayer and fasting. If you, therefore, practice sobriety and purity in patience and humility of heart, the Lord will dwell among you, because He loves

Testament of Joseph

sobriety. Wherever the Most High dwells, even though a man falls into envy, slavery, or slander, the Lord who dwells in him, for his sobriety's sake, not only delivers him from evil, but also exalts and glorifies him, even as me. For in every way the man is guarded, whether in deed, or in word, or in thought. My brothers, know how my father loved me, and I was not exalted in my heart. Although I was a child, I had the fear of God in my thoughts. For I knew that all things should pass away, and I kept myself within bounds, and I honored my brothers. Through fear of them I held my peace when I was sold, and revealed not my family to the Ishmaelites, that I was the son of Jacob, a great and mighty man.

11. The Fear of God

"Do you also, therefore, have the fear of God in your works, and honor your family? For everyone who follows the law of the Lord will be loved by Him. When I came to the Indocolpitæ with the Ishmaelites, they asked me, and I said that I was a slave from their house, that I might not put my brothers to shame. The eldest of them said unto me, 'You are not a slave, even your appearance shows that.' He threatened to kill me, but I said that I was their slave. Now when we came into Egypt, they strove concerning me, which of them should buy me and take me. Therefore, it seemed good to all that I should remain in Egypt with a merchant of their trade, until they should return bringing merchandise. The Lord gave me favor in the eyes of the merchant, and he entrusted to me his house. The Lord blessed him because of me, and increased him in silver and gold, and I was with him three months and five days.

12. God and Your Reputation
"About that time the Memphian wife of Potiphar passed by with great pomp, and cast her eyes upon me, because her eunuchs told her concerning me. She told her husband concerning the merchant, that he had become rich by means of a young Hebrew, saying, 'They say that men have indeed stolen him out of the land of Canaan. Now therefore execute judgment with him, and take away the youth to be your steward; so, the God of the Hebrews will bless you, for grace from heaven is upon him.'

13. Joseph in Egypt
"Potiphar was persuaded by her words, and commanded the merchant to be brought, and said unto him, 'What is this that I hear, that you steal people out of the land of the Hebrews, and sell them for slaves?' The merchant therefore fell upon his face, and besought him, saying, 'I beseech you, my lord, I know not what you say.' He said, 'From where then is your Hebrew servant?' He said, 'The Ishmaelites entrusted him to me until they should return.' He believed him not, but commanded him to be stripped and beaten. When he persisted, Potiphar said, 'Let the youth be brought.' When I was brought in, I did obeisance to the chief of the eunuchs — for he was third in rank with Pharaoh, being chief of all the eunuchs, and having wives and children and concubines. He took me apart from him, and said unto me, 'Are you a slave or free?' I said, 'A slave.' He said unto me, 'Whose slave are you?' I

said to him, 'The Ishmaelites'.' Again he said to me, 'How did you become their slave?' I said, 'They bought me out of the land of Canaan.' But he did not believe me, and said, 'You lie,' and he commanded me to be stripped and beaten.

14. Memphian Woman Tries to Obtain Joseph
"Now the Memphian woman was looking through a window while I was being beaten, and she sent unto her husband, saying, 'Your judgment is unjust; for you punish a free man who has been stolen, as if he were a transgressor.' When I gave no other answer though I was beaten, he commanded that I should be kept in guard, until, said he, 'the owners of the boy should come.' His wife said unto him, 'Why do you detain in captivity this noble child, who ought rather to be set at liberty, and wait upon you?' For she wished to see me in desire of sin, but I was ignorant concerning all these things. Then he said to his wife, 'It is not the custom of the Egyptians to take away that which belongs to others before proof is given.' This he said concerning the merchant, and concerning me, that I must be imprisoned.

15. Joseph with the Ishmaelites
"Now, after twenty-four days the Ishmaelites came. Having heard that Jacob my father was mourning for me, they said to me, 'Why did you say that you were a slave? We have learned that you are the son of a mighty man in the land of Canaan, and your father grieves for you in sackcloth.' I would have wept again, but I restrained myself, that I should not put my brothers to shame. I said,

'I do not know; I am a slave.' Then they took counsel to sell me, so that I would not be found in their hands. For they feared Jacob, lest he should work upon them a deadly vengeance. For it had been heard that he was mighty with the Lord and with men. Then the merchant said to them, 'Release me from the judgment of Potiphar.' They therefore came and asked for me, saying, 'He was bought by us with money.' And he sent us away.

16. Joseph Bought

"Now the Memphian woman pointed me out to her husband, that he should buy me; 'for I hear,' she said, 'that they are selling him.' She sent a eunuch to the Ishmaelites, and asked them to sell me; and since he was not willing to traffic with them, he returned. When the eunuch had made trial of them, he made known to his mistress that they asked a large price for their slave. She sent another eunuch, saying, 'Even if they demand two minæ of gold, do not to spare the gold; only buy the boy, and bring him here.' He gave them eighty pieces of gold for me, and told his mistress that a hundred had been given for me. When I saw it I held my peace, that the eunuch should not be punished.

17. Forgive Those Who Wrong You

"My children, you see what great things I endured that I should not put my brothers to shame. Do you also love one another, and with patience hide one another's faults? For God delights in the unity of families, and in the purpose of a heart approved unto love. When my brothers came into Egypt, and learned that I returned their money unto them, and did not accuse them, instead I comforted them, and after the death of Jacob I loved them all the more. And everything that he commanded I did very abundantly, then they marveled. For I did not allow them to be afflicted even to the smallest matter; and all that was in my hand I gave to them. Their children were my children, and my children were as their servants. Their life was my life, all their suffering was my suffering, and all their sickness was my infirmity. My land was their land, my counsel their counsel, and I did not exalt myself among them in arrogance because of my worldly glory, but I was among them as one of the least.

18. Walk in the Ways of the Lord

"If you walk in the commandments of the Lord, my children, He will exalt you there, and will bless you with good things forever and ever. If anyone seeks to do evil to you, pray for him, and you will be redeemed of the Lord from all evil. You see that through patience I took a wife, even the daughter of my master. A hundred talents of gold were given me with her; for the Lord made them to serve me. He gave me also beauty as a flower above the beautiful ones of Israel. He preserved me to old age in strength and in beauty, because I was like in all things to Jacob.

19. Joseph's Visions

"Hear also, my children, the visions which I saw. There were twelve deer feeding, and the nine were divided and scattered in the land, likewise also the three. I saw that from Judah was born a virgin wearing a linen garment, and from her went forth a Lamb, without spot, and on His left hand there was a lion. All the beasts rushed against Him, and the Lamb overcame them, destroyed them, and trampled them under foot. Because of Him, the angels, men, and all the earth rejoiced. These things will take place in their season, in the last days. Therefore, my children, observe the commandments of the Lord, and honor Judah and Levi. From them will rise unto you the Lamb of God, by grace saving all the Gentiles and Israel. For His kingdom is an everlasting kingdom, which will not be shaken; but my kingdom among you will come to an end as a watcher's hammock, which after the summer will not appear.

20. Joseph's Death
"I know that after my death the Egyptians will afflict you, but God will undertake your cause, and will bring you into that which He promised to your fathers. But carry my bones up with you; for when my bones are taken up, the Lord will be with you in light, and Belial will be in darkness with the Egyptians. Carry up Zilpah, your mother, and lay her near Bilhah, by the hippodrome, by the side of Rachel."

When he had said these things, he stretched out his feet, and slept the long sleep. All Israel and Egypt mourned him with a great lamentation, for he felt for the Egyptians even as his own family, and showed them kindness, aiding them in every work, counsel, and matter.

Testament of Joseph

4Q539

4Q539 is five very small fragments of the Testament of Joseph. Phrases like "my uncle Ishmael" are readable.

Commentary

Joseph 19 reveals that the Messiah will be virgin-born.

Testament of Benjamin

Concerning a Pure Mind.

1. Benjamin

The record of the words of Benjamin, which he set forth to his sons, after he had lived a hundred and twenty years. He kissed them, and said, "As Isaac was born to Abraham in his hundredth year, so also was I to Jacob. Since Rachel died in giving me birth, I had no milk. Therefore, I was nursed by Bilhah her handmaid. Rachel remained barren for twelve years after she gave birth to Joseph. She prayed to the Lord with fasting for twelve days, and she conceived and bare me. Our father loved Rachel dearly, and prayed that he might see two sons born from her; which is why I was called the son of days, which is Benjamin.

2. Benjamin and Joseph

"When I went into Egypt, and Joseph my brother recognized me, he asked me, 'What did they tell my father when they sold me?' I said unto him, 'They dabbled your coat with blood and sent it, and said, 'Is this the coat of your son?' He said to me, 'When the Ishmaelites took me, one of them stripped off my coat, gave me a girdle, scourged me, and told me to run. As he went away to hide my garment, a lion met him and killed him; and so, his partners were afraid, and sold me to their companions.'

Testament of Benjamin

3. Godliness Protects from Evil

"My children, love the Lord God of heaven, and keep His commandments, and be followers of the good and holy man Joseph. Let your mind focus on what is good, as I do. He that focuses on good sees all things correctly. Fear the Lord, and love your neighbor. Even if the spirits of Belial allure you into troublesome wickedness, yet it will have no dominion over you, just as it did not over Joseph my brother. How many men wished to kill him, and God shielded him! He who fears God and loves his neighbor cannot be afflicted by Belial's spirit of the air, being shielded by the fear of God. Neither can he be ruled over by the device of men or of beasts, for he is aided by the love of the Lord which he has towards his neighbor. Joseph even asked our father Jacob to pray for our brothers, that the Lord would not impute to them the evil that they devised concerning Joseph. Thus, Jacob cried out, 'My child Joseph, you have touched the heart of your father Jacob.' He embraced him, and kissed him for two hours, saying, 'In you will be fulfilled the prophecy of heaven concerning the Lamb of God, even the Savior of the world. He will be delivered up spotless for transgressors. He will be sinless, yet put to death for ungodly men in the blood of the covenant, for the salvation of the Gentiles and of Israel. He will destroy Belial, and them that serve him.'

4. Godly Men

"My children, you know what happens to a godly man. Follow his compassion with a good mind, that you also may wear crowns of glory. The good man does not have a dark eye. He shows mercy to all men, even though they are sinners, even though they devise evil against him. So, he who does good overcomes the evil, being shielded by Him who is good. He loves the righteous as his own soul. If anyone is glorified, he does not envy him. If anyone is enriched, he is not jealous. If anyone is valiant, he praises him. He trusts and praises the sober-minded. He shows mercy to the poor. He helps the weak. He sings the praises of God. He protects those who fear God, like a shield. He aides those who love God, but warns and turns away those who reject God. He loves those who have the grace of God, like his own soul.

5. The Power of Forgiveness
"If you have a good mind, my children, then wicked men will be at peace with you. The profligate will reverence you and turn to good. The covetous will not only stop being greedy, but start giving to those who are afflicted. If you do well, the unclean spirits will flee from you. Even beasts will flee from you in dread. Darkness flees from those who reverence good works. When anyone injures a holy man, they repent because the holy man forgives him and holds his peace. If anyone betrays a righteous soul, the righteous man, though praying, may be humbled for a little while. Yet, not long afterwards he appears far more glorious, as Joseph my brother did.

6. The Godly Mind
"The mind of the good man is not under the power of the deceit of the spirit of Belial, for the angel of peace guides his soul. He does not gaze passionately on corruptible

Testament of Benjamin

things, nor hoard riches for his own pleasure. He does not delight in pleasure, hurt his neighbor, pamper himself with food, or err in pride, for the Lord is his portion. The good mind does not dwell on the glory or dishonor of men. He does not practice guile, lying, fighting, or reviling. The Lord dwells with him and lights up his soul, and he rejoices with all men. The good mind is not hypocritical. It does not bless and curse, insult and honor, or spread sorrow and joy. It does not make peace and cause trouble, speak hypocritically and truthfully, or bring poverty and wealth. It only has one temperament: pure and uncorrupt, concerning all men. It has no trouble seeing and hearing the truth, for in everything the Lord watches his soul, and keeps his mind clean so that he will not be condemned by God or men. But every work of Belial is hypocritical, and cannot be straight.

7. Sin Caused by not Trusting God

"My children, flee Belial's temptation to sin, for it brings a sword to those who obey, and the sword causes seven evils. When the mind first conceives sin, it brings envy, ruin, tribulation, exile, need, panic, and destruction. Cain received seven judgments by God, for in every hundred years the Lord brought one plague upon him. When he was two hundred he began to suffer and when he was nine hundred he was destroyed for Abel his righteous brother's sake. Cain was judged seven hundred years, and Lamech, seventy times seven.[bbb] All those who are like Cain in

---

[bbb] This sentence is confusing.

their envy and hatred will always be punished in the same way.

8. The Pure Mind
"Therefore, my children, flee all wrong-doing, envy, and hatred of family, and cleave to goodness and love. He who has a pure mind in love does not think about fornicating with a woman because he has no defilement in his heart, and the Spirit of God rests in him just as the sun is not defiled by shining over dung and mire, but rather it dries up both and drives away the stench. So also, the pure mind, constrained among the defilements of the earth, rather edifies others and suffers no defilement itself.

9. Rebellion Against the Messiah
"The words of the righteous Enoch teach that even your descendants will practice evil. They will commit fornication like the fornication of Sodom, and all but a few will perish, and will multiply inordinate lusts with women; and the kingdom of the Lord will not be among you, for immediately He will take it away. Nevertheless, the temple of God will be built in your portion, and will be glorious among you. For He will take it, and the twelve tribes will be gathered together there, and all the Gentiles, until the Most High will send forth His salvation in the visitation of His only-begotten One. He will enter into the front of the temple, and there will the Lord be treated with outrage, and He will be lifted up on a tree. The veil of the temple will be rent, and the Spirit of God will descend upon the Gentiles as fire poured forth. He will rise from the grave, and will ascend from earth into heaven. I know

Testament of Benjamin

how lowly He will be upon the earth, and how glorious in the heaven.

10. The Inheritance

"Now when Joseph was in Egypt, I longed to see him face to face; and through the prayers of Jacob my father I saw him, while awake in the daytime, in his full and perfect shape. Know therefore, my children, that I am dying. Work truth and righteousness to your neighbors, judge righteously, and keep the law of the Lord and His commandments. These things I teach you instead of an inheritance. Give them also to your children for an everlasting possession; for so did Abraham, Isaac, and Jacob. These things they gave us for an inheritance, saying, 'Keep the commandments of God until the Lord will reveal His salvation to all nations.' Then you will see Enoch, Noah, Shem, Abraham, Isaac, and Jacob, rising on the right hand in gladness. Then we will also rise, each one over our tribe, worshipping the King of Heaven, who appeared upon the earth in the form of a man of humility. All those who believed on Him on the earth will rejoice with Him; and then will all men arise, some unto glory and some unto shame. The Lord will judge Israel first, even for the wrong they did unto Him; for when He appeared as a deliverer, God in the flesh, they did not believe Him. Then He will judge all the Gentiles, as many as did not believe Him when He appeared on earth. He will reprove Israel among the chosen ones of the Gentiles, even as He reproved Esau among the Midianites, who deceived their brothers, so that they fell into fornication and idolatry. They were alienated from God, and became as those who were not children in the portion of them that fear the Lord. But if you walk in holiness in the presence of the Lord, you will dwell in hope again with me, and all Israel will be gathered unto the Lord.

11. Prophecy of the Apostle Paul

"I will no longer be called a ravening wolf on account of your ravages, but a worker of the Lord, distributing food to them that work what is good. One will rise up from my seed in the latter times, beloved of the Lord, hearing His voice on the earth, enlightening with new knowledge all the Gentiles, bursting in on Israel for salvation with the light of knowledge, and tearing it away from them like a wolf, and giving it to the synagogue of the Gentiles. Until the consummation of the ages he[ccc] will be in the synagogues of the Gentiles, and among their rulers, as a strain of music in the mouth of all; and he will be inscribed in the holy books, both his work and his word, and he will be a chosen one of God forever; and because of him my father Jacob instructed me, saying, 'He will fill up that which lacks from your tribe.'"

12. Benjamin's Death

When he finished his words, he said: "I charge you, my children, carry up my bones out of Egypt, and bury me at Hebron, near my fathers." So, Benjamin died a hundred and twenty-five years old, in a good old age, and they placed him in a coffin. In the ninety-first year of the

---

[ccc] The apostle Paul's writings will be included in the Scriptures forever.

Testament of Benjamin

departure of the children of Israel from Egypt, they and their brothers brought up the bones of their fathers secretly in a place which is called Canaan; and they buried them in Hebron, by the feet of their fathers. They returned from the land of Canaan, and lived in Egypt until the day of their departing from the land of Egypt.

Commentary

Benjamin 3 predicts that the Messiah would be sinless, and bring salvation to the whole world by being put to death by godless men.

Benjamin 9 predicts the temple will be built in the tribe of Benjamin. The temple ceases when the Messiah brings His salvation. The Messiah will be crucified and the veil of the temple will be rent.

Benjamin 10 teaches the Messiah will be God in flesh and that all men will resurrect.

Benjamin 11 describes the apostle Paul and his written works making up most of what we call the New Testament.

Testament of Kohath

4Q542

Fragment 1

"…and God of gods for all the centuries. He will make His light shine upon you and you will know His great name. …you will know Him, because He is the God of the centuries, the Lord of all creation, and the Ruler of all, to deal with them as He wishes. He will create great joy and gladness for you and your sons in the generations of truth forever. Now, my sons, be careful with the inheritance which has been given to you by our fathers. Do not give your inheritance to foreigners or your heritage to half-breeds, or you will become foolishly humiliated in their eyes. They will scorn you when they go from being residents among you to being chiefs over you. Hold on to the words of our righteous fathers: Abraham, Jacob, Levi, and my words. Be holy and pure from all corruption. Hold on to the truth and walk in uprightness. Do not be double-minded, but have a pure heart and a truthful and good spirit. It will give a good name to me, joy to Levi, gladness to Jacob, rejoicing to Isaac, and honor to Abraham; if you keep and carry on the inheritance which your fathers gave you in truth, justice, uprightness, perfection, purity, and holiness. You must keep the priesthood in every way that I have commanded you and according to all that…

Testament of Kohath

Fragment 2

"...I have taught you in truth. Now, and for all time, the word of truth will come on you and eternal blessings will rest on you and will be... will remain throughout all generations and there will be no more... from your punishment, and you will rise to make judgement on... and to see the sins of all the sinners of the world... in the fire, in the abyss, and in all the caverns in order to... in the time of justice; and all the wicked will vanish. Now, Amram, my son, I command you and your descendants... given to Levi my father, which he in turn gave to me along with all my writings as witness. You must take care of them. They are for you and your descendants and in them is great worth. It is important that they be carried on with you.

Fragment 3

"... to read and... his sons... men and life...upon them and... darkness and... and light, but... and I... the stones were heavy... will be great in number because of fornication. Those who... very great, because very few..."

Commentary

Fragment 1 of the *Testament of Kohath* seems to be saying that God would bless his children, specifically the descendants of his grandson Levi, the priests. Even though the Levitical priests did not inherit land, they inherit something. The inheritance that Kohath is referring to is most likely the testaments of their fathers: all the books and prophecies from Adam down to Kohath. The Talmud testifies that these books were given to Levi and his descendants to keep for all generations. The idea that some might try to kill the Messiah before He was fully grown probably lead to the tradition that these writings should be kept secret in order to protect Him.

Fragment 2 seems to state that the priesthood will bring in the everlasting kingdom but some of the priests would be wicked. Levi and the righteous priests will rise and judge those who transgressed. This sounds like the apostle Paul when he said we would "judge the angels." Kohath then tells his descendants how important it is to preserve the written records of the fathers. Levi gave them to him and he now hands them over to Amram for his posterity.

Fragment 3 is so badly fragmented that all we can glean from it is that fornication is very evil. He may have been telling of a dream about God destroying fornicators with giant falling stones, a type of wrath from heaven.

Testament of Amram

4Q543 - 4Q549

4Q543

...copy of the book of the words of the vision of Amram, son of Kohath, son of Levi, all that he explained to his sons on his deathbed. He was one hundred and thirty-seven years old when he died, which was the one hundred and fifty-second year of Israel's exile in Egypt. He should ... "...to call Uzziel, his youngest brother, and he gave his thirty-year-old daughter, Miriam, to him for a wife. He gave a wedding feast lasting seven days. He ate, drank, and rejoiced during the feast. When the days of the wedding feast were over, he called for Aaron, his son, who was about twenty years old, and told him, 'Son, call the messengers, your brothers from the house of ...'

4Q544

"Kohath went there to stay, dwell, and build ... many of the sons of my uncle together with... since the work was very great and would continue until our dead would be buried there... In the year when I began, news of a war brewing worried me. I allowed those of our company who wanted to return to Egypt to go and I went on to finish the work and to bury them. They did not help in finishing the tombs of our fathers. My father Kohath, and my wife, Jochebed, left me to stay and build, and provide them with all their needs from the land of Canaan. We dwelt in

Hebron while we were building. A war broke out between the Philistines and the Egyptians. When the Philistines defeated the Egyptians with the help of the Canaanites, they closed off the border of Egypt. It was impossible for Jochebed, my wife, to come here to Canaan from Egypt for forty-one years. We could not return to Egypt either. We could not even... the Egyptian and Canaanite / Philistine War... During all this time, I was separated from Jochebed, my wife, who was in Egypt ... I in Canaan ... for she was not with me. I did not take another wife... Women... All I ever thought about was returning to Egypt in peace to see the face of my wife.

4Q545

"I had a dream where I saw two Watchers. They were arguing about me, saying... it became a heated argument about me. I asked them why... They answered me, 'We have been made masters of the earth and rule over all the nations of men.' Then they asked me, 'Which one of us do you choose ...' I looked closely at one of them and he looked frightening, like a serpent, and he wore multi-colored clothes, but he was extremely dark... I looked at the other and... his face looked like an adder covered with... both together, and over his eyes...

4Q546

"...this Watcher, 'Who is he?' He answered me saying, 'This Watcher... and his three names are Belial, Prince of

Testament of Amram

Darkness, and Melkiresha'[ddd] I said: 'My Lord, what rule ...' He said to me... '... and all of his paths and all of his works only lead to darkness, and he is... in darkness... He rules over all darkness ... and I rule over all light and all...'

4Q547

"... and I will explain to you your names... that he wrote for Moses, and also about Aaron... I will explain to you the mystery of His worship. He is a holy priest to the Most High God. Also, all of his seed will be holy throughout their generations, eternally... The seventh of the men of (God's) good will he will be called and he will be said ... and will be chosen as a priest forever...

4Q548

"...I declare the true path to you. I will instruct you... the sons of light will teach truth, and all the sons of darkness will teach deceit. By their knowledge all the sons of light will... but the sons of darkness will be removed... Every wicked fool will flee to the darkness but every righteous sage will seek the light. For all the sons of light will be drawn to the light, but all the sons of darkness will be drawn to death and destruction... They will explain the light to the people..."

[ddd] King of Rosh, see Ezekiel 38.

Ancient Testaments of the Patriarchs

Commentary

4Q543 stated that Miriam, the sister of Moses, was married at the age of 30. From the Bible, we know she married Hur.

4Q544 tells that Kohath and a team of cousins went to build the sepulchers at the cave of Macpelah. This is where Sarah and Abraham are buried. A war broke out and the border of Egypt and Canaan was closed for forty-one years. Amram was separated from Jochebed, his wife, all this time. This same thing happened to many Germans while the Berlin wall was up the 28 years, from 1961 to 1989. This story is significant because a legend in the Talmud says Amram divorced his wife. We see here that he never did. Although this error in the Talmud is very understandable under this circumstance, it shows that not everything in the Talmud is true.

4Q545-4Q546 related a dream Amram had about Watchers who were fighting over him for domination of the nations of earth.

4Q547 seems to be teaching the Talmudic legend that all the names of the patriarchs, from Adam through Aaron, are themselves prophetic. He goes further stating that there is a prophetic mystery in the worship rituals and the generations. He then seems to be saying that the seventh from Adam (Enoch) would preserve the teachings for all time. This is either referring to the book of Enoch and/or the writings his forefathers (Adam through Jared).

4Q548 teaches godly people will be drawn to the truth of God's word and desire to study and understand and teach others about Him. Evil people will try to convince others they are righteous, but their deeds will expose them because they have no love for Scriptures.

Testament of Aaron

AARON A – 4Q540-4Q541

Column 1, Fragment 2

"...words... and according to the will of... to me. Once more he wrote... I spoke about them in parables... was close to me. Therefore, ... was far away from me... The vision will be profound... the fruit...

Column 1, Fragment 6

"... deep things... those who do not understand. He wrote... and he calmed the great sea... Then the books of wisdom will be opened... by his word...

Column 2

"... God... You will receive the afflicted... will bless their burnt offerings and You will establish for them a foundation of Your peace... your spirit, and you will rejoice in your God. Now I am speaking to you in parables... rejoice. Behold, wise men will understand the visions and comprehend the deep mysteries, which is why I speak in parables. The Greek... [non-God fearer] will never understand. But the knowledge of wisdom will come to you, for you have received... you will acquire... Pursue wisdom and continue to seek her. Let her become a part of you. Behold, you will make many glad and give them a place...

Testament of Aaron

Column 4

"... His wisdom will be great. He will make atonement for all the children of His generation. He will be sent to all the sons of His [generation]. His word will be as the word of heaven, and His teaching will be in accordance with the will of God. His eternal sun will burn bright. The fire will be kindled in all the corners of the earth. It will shine into the darkness. Then the darkness will vanish from the earth and the deep darkness from the dry land. They will speak many words against Him. There will be numerous lies. They will invent stories about Him. They will say shameful things about Him. He will overthrow His evil generation and there will be great wrath. When He arises, there will be falsehood and violence, and the people will wander astray in His days and be confounded.

Column 5, Fragment 1

"I saw one... I saw seven rams... Some of his sons will walk... They will be gathered to the heavenly beings...

Column 5, Fragment 5

"...and those who are grieved about... your judgment but you will not be guilty... the scourging of those who afflict you... your complaint will not fail and all... your heart...

Column 6

"God will right all the errors... He will reveal and judge sins... Learn fully why Jonah wept. ...will not destroy the weak by wasting away or by crucifixion... Let not the nail touch him. Then you will raise up for your father a name of rejoicing and for all your brothers a firm foundation.

You will understand and rejoice in the eternal light and you will not be one whom God hates."

Commentary

Columns 1 and 2 seem to be about a dream where Aaron needs to be schooled in God's wisdom (from the books of his fathers) to understand the parables in dreams and visions. Those who do not try to study prophecy will never get to a place where they can understand the things of God.

Column 4 seems to continue with a description of the Messiah. When He comes, Aaron's descendants will turn on Him with lies and violence. Those who reject Messiah will wander in confusion.

Column 5 seems to be a part of a vision where Aaron's descendants are divided into seven categories. Some walk in a godly manner and others do not. The godly will be "gathered" to heaven.

Column 6 continues teaching about Messiah. God will right all the errors through Him by crucifixion. If you do not want to be hated by God, accept Him and have no part in His crucifixion.

Prophecy Outline

> Messiah is the Son of God (L4)
> Messiah is God incarnate (S6,7; Z9; N8; As7; B10)
> Levi's priesthood is only until Messiah (R6; L4,5; B9)
> Levi's ordinances and sacrifices are only until Messiah (R6)
> Tribes rebel against Judah and Levi (R6; D5)
> Messiah is the seed of Judah (R6; Ju24; G8)
> Messiah is virgin-born (Jo19)
> We worship the Messiah (R6)
> Messiah is an everlasting King (R6; Jo19)
> Messiah dies for us (R6)
> Physical resurrection (S6; Ju25; Z10; B10)
> Messiah brings salvation (S6; L4; As7; Jo19; B3)
> Levites crucify the Messiah (L4,16; Aa4,6; B9)
> There will be two expulsions (L15; Z9; N4; As7)
> Messiah resurrects (L16)
> Messiah ascends (L18)
> Messiah creates a new priesthood (L18; Aa4)
> *Book of Enoch* mentioned (L16; Ju18; Z3; N4; B9)
> The *Writings of the Fathers* existed (Z9; K2)
> Messiah appears in Zebulun (Z9)
> New Jerusalem mentioned (D5)
> Old Jerusalem mentioned (Ja2)
> The Watchers mentioned (N3)
> Messiah's priesthood is eternal (Am-4Q547; Aa4)
> Veil of the Temple Rent (B9)

Legend: **Ja**cob, **R**euben, **S**imeon, **L**evi, **Ju**dah, **I**ssachar, **Z**ebulun, **D**an, **N**aphtali, **G**ad, **As**her, **Jo**seph, **B**enjamin, **K**ohath, **Am**ram, **Aa**ron

The Messianic prophecies that occur numerous times throughout the testaments are given in the above chart. Now we want to focus our attention on the more complex prophecies.

Levi 4 seems to teach that the prophecy in Genesis 12:3 refers to the Messiah.

> "And I will bless them that bless thee, and curse him that curseth thee: and in thee will all families of the earth be blessed." *Genesis 12:3*

Levi instructs his sons to teach about the coming Messiah that those who

> "bless Him will be blessed, but those who curse Him will perish."

In Levi 8, Levi is given a prophecy in which he is told that there will be three different priesthoods. The last one is a priesthood that the Messiah brings. It states the Messiah will be a:

> "King from Judah, and will establish a new priesthood, after the fashion of the Gentiles, to all the Gentiles."

This sounds like somewhere in the genealogy Jesus is not only a direct descendant of Judah through David but also a descendant of Levi. Elisabeth, the mother of John the Baptist, was a Levite and she was also a cousin of Mary, Jesus' mother.

Levi 18 teaches the Messiah's children (true believers) will have power over evil spirits.

Benjamin 9 states that the Messiah is the only begotten of God and He will be lifted up on a tree. The Essenes were to look for the sign of the veil in the temple being supernaturally rent, or torn in two. This was foretold to be a sign that the priesthood had rejected the Messiah and that God was then rejecting the priesthood. Once the Essenes saw the fulfillment of that particular sign, they no longer offered sacrifices in the Jerusalem temple. The Messiah was to be buried, resurrect, and ascend. Afterwards, the Spirit of God would be poured out on all believers (Gentiles included) in the form of fire.

Judah 24 says the Messiah is a root of Jacob (called a star, branch, and rod) and the ruler over the righteous Gentiles, saving everyone who calls on the Lord.

Simeon 7 teaches that the Messiah will be both king and priest; but says it in such a way that you cannot tell if it is two messiahs, or one messiah who holds both offices simultaneously. We know now that it was one messiah holding two offices. This might have been the reason that some first century BC rabbis thought there would be two messiahs: King Messiah, a son of David, and Priest Messiah, a son of Joseph.

Amram (4Q547) gives the impression that the names of the patriarchs are themselves a prophecy and starts to reveal what their names mean (including Moses and Aaron) and how they relate to the Messiah's priesthood. He then reveals that Enoch, the seventh from Adam, preserved the prophecies and history in his book and the books of his forefathers.

Naphtali 5 predicts that there will be seven kingdoms that will rule over Israel until the time of the Messiah. These are listed as the Assyrians, Medes, Persians, [Elamites, Gelachæans,] Chaldeans, and Syrians. The Elamites and Gelachæans are not listed in some manuscripts. We know that Israel was ruled over by Egypt, Assyria, Babylon, the Medes and Persians together, the Grecian Seludian kingdom headquartered in Syria, and then Rome. They will later be ruled over by the ten nations described in Daniel and Revelation.

According the Geoffrey Keating, one of the few surviving Gaelic historians, the Gaelic and Hebrew languages were very similar right after the fall of the tower of Babel. See *Ancient Post-Flood History*, chapter 13 for details. The word "Gelach" in Gaelic means the moon. So, in this vision, Gelachæans could mean "moon people." This is significant because a very similar prophecy is found in the *Book of Gad the Seer*, chapters 1-2. In those chapters the moon represents the Jewish kingdom, which is usurped by two anti-Semitic powers represented by a donkey and camel. These are defined as the end times religious powers of Islam and Roman Catholicism.

Could the ten nations of Daniel and Revelation be comprised of nations that are strictly Roman Catholic and Islamic?

The Jubilee Prophecy

One of the most interesting prophecies is given in Levi 16-17. Levi 16 states that there is a seventy-weeks prophecy given in the book of Enoch, which we do not have. During this four hundred and ninety years, all of Israel will go astray. The priesthood will become profane, the sacrifices polluted, and the law corrupted. The four gospels show that the priesthood was indeed corrupt and the law was twisted into what the corrupt priesthood wanted it to mean. Many times Jesus rebuked the Sadducees and Pharisees over these kinds of issues. They did call the Messiah a deceiver. Jesus was crucified and the nation of Israel was desolated.

Levi 17 shows the specifics of how and when this would happen. The school of Elijah taught human time was divided into three sets of two-thousand-year periods known as ages. There was the age of Chaos, from Creation to the call of Abraham. The second age was called the age of Torah, extending from the call of Abraham to the dissolving of the sacrificial system. The third age was called the Messianic age. Christians call this the Church Age. After the Messianic age, there was to be a one-thousand-year period of a Messianic Kingdom. Christians call this the Millennial Reign. Each age is broken up into periods of five-hundred years called Onahs (see the Hebrew commentary on the Epistle of Elijah entitled the Tana Eliyahu for details). Levi described the events that occur in the last five-hundred-year period of the age of Torah. It is divided into ten jubilees of fifty years each. In the last jubilee of the previous five-hundred-year period, Nehemiah (Nehemiah 2:1-8) gained permission from Artaxerxes to rebuild Jerusalem. This was in 444 BC. Here is a timetable for the jubilees from Levi 17.

Jub.	Date	
	587 BC	1st Temple Destroyed
	517 BC	2nd Temple Dedicated
	444 BC	Artaxerxes' decree (70 weeks prophecy – Daniel 9)
1	425-375 BC	
2	375-325 BC	
3	325-275 BC	
4	275-225 BC	
5	225-175 BC	
6	175-125 BC	Antiochus Epiphanes 163 BC
7	125-75 BC	Week five, 96-89 BC – Civil War Week seven, 82-75 BC – Corrupt priests arise
8	75-25 BC	Herod the Great 37 BC
9	25 BC - 25 AD	
10	25-75 AD	Week one, AD 25-32 Messiah crucified AD 32 Week seven, AD 68-75 Sacrifices abolished ~ Council of Yavneh AD 75

The important thing to note is that the priesthood was restored after the Babylonian captivity, but began to fall apart jubilee by jubilee. He predicts some form of war, dispersion, and a return to sanctify the temple in the fifth week of the seventh Jubilee. This fifth week is exactly the same time period as the civil war between the Sadducees and Pharisees.

We know we have the jubilees dated correctly, not only because it agrees with the timetable of the destruction of

Jubilee Prophecy

Solomon's temple being 3338AM and 587 BC, but because of another Dead Sea Scroll called the 11QMelchizedek (see next chapter for the translation). In column 2 of this work, it states that the coming Messiah will fulfill several prophecies, including when Daniel 9 says He would come. It says, "This event will take place in the first week of the jubilee that occurs after the ninth jubilee." In AD 70 the Jerusalem temple was destroyed. In AD 73 Titus destroyed the Jewish temple in Alexandria, Egypt (see Josephus Wars 7). Two years later, in AD 75, we have the first council of Yavneh where the Sanhedrin ruled that there was no more need for a temple and sacrificial system. God put it into their hearts to end an age as He predicted! Now, AD 75 minus a fifty-year jubilee would bring the close of the ninth jubilee to AD 25. One Shemittah (week of years) later would be (25+7) AD 32, the year the Messiah was crucified!

It is most important that we focus on weeks five and seven of the seventh jubilee. After Judah Maccabee led the successful revolt against Antiochus Epiphanes in 165 BC, his successors started the Hasmonean Dynasty. When both the Seleucid and Roman Empires recognized Israel as an independent nation in 110 BC, John Hyrcanus started a campaign of conquest of neighboring nations. He ruled as king and high priest which was forbidden. The Jews who supported the high priest king and the idea of priestly rule became known as Sadducees. Their name was taken from Zadok the priest. Dissenters arose who believed the king did not have the right to force non-Jews to convert to Judaism and be circumcised. They were known as separatists, or Pharisees in Hebrew.

In 103 BC, Alexander Jannaeus became the next Hasmonean ruler. He not only continued the idea of priestly rule and forcing all Jews and Gentiles to be circumcised, but all Jews and Gentiles must follow the priestly code. This command led to the Pharisees' rebellion. The Pharisees believed that the law of priests was only meant for priests and not common Jews or Gentiles. They said the king had no right to force conversion or require non-priests to follow the priestly code. This plunged Israel in to an eight-year civil war, from 96-88 BC.

During the intense persecution of the Pharisees, Simeon ben Shetach, a Pharisee and Nasi (president of the Sanhedrin), fled to safety in Alexandria, Egypt, where he met two men Shmya and Abtalion, who were natives of Alexandria, but direct descendants of the king of Assyria. They were converted to Judaism. The persecution ended; and he returned to Jerusalem. When his sister, Queen Salome of Alexandria, became the next Hasmonean Ruler, Simeon and the Pharisees became very powerful. Simeon ben Shetach started mandatory Torah schools replacing the long-standing rule that the fathers teach their sons the Torah. All children were required to attend these schools for proper indoctrination. He then brought his two Assyrian converts to Jerusalem and they succeeded him as rulers in the Sanhedrin. They changed the standard way of interpreting Torah and replaced it with what would

Jubilee Prophecy

become known as Midrashic interpretation. They were the first "Darshan", or preachers. Their new method of Torah interpretation was called "Derush," or oral tradition. From this point forward, legal rulings of the Sanhedrin were binding on all, and were to be enforced for all future generations.

A new denomination emerged from this called the Essenes. They agreed with the Pharisees that forced conversion and forced observance of the priestly code by non-priests was wrong. However, they disagreed with the new doctrine that the tradition of "Oral Torah" was equal to the written Torah. They believed no one had the power to go against the written Torah and the written histories of the forefathers.

Levi 17 says in the seventh week priests would come that would bring great corruption. Dead Sea Scroll 4Q385a says that this would be three priests, and 4Q387 says that by the end of the tenth jubilee, "all of Israel would be walking in madness." I believe these priests were Simeon ben Shetach, Shmya, and Abtalion.

Related Dead Sea Scrolls

The following Dead Sea Scrolls provide a more in-depth look at Bible prophecy from the Essenes' point of view. Like Christians, Essenes believed these prophecies are fulfilled by the Messiah. Pharisees disagreed.

11QMelchizedek Column 2
"Moses said, 'In the year of the jubilee, each of you will be freed to return home [Lev. 25:13]' and he described how, saying, 'Now this is the manner of the release: Let every creditor remit what he has lent his neighbor. He shall not press his neighbor or his brother for repayment, for the LORD's release has been proclaimed [Deut. 15:2].' Its interpretation pertains to the end of days. The captives Moses speaks of are those whom Isaiah says 'To proclaim freedom to the captives [Isa 61:1].' Its interpretation is that the LORD will assign those freed to the sons of heaven and the lot of Melchizedek. Even those, whose teachers had deliberately hidden and kept secret from them the truth about their inheritance through Melchizedek. The LORD will cast their lot amid the portions of Melchizedek, who will make them return [or repent] and will proclaim freedom to them, to free them from the debt of all their iniquities. This event will take place in the first week of the jubilee that occurs after the ninth jubilee.

"Now the Day of Atonement is the end of the tenth jubilee, when atonement (is made) for all the sons of heaven, for the men of the lot of Melchizedek... It is the time of Melchizedek's 'Day of Grace.' He will, by His strength, raise up the holy ones of God to execute judgment as it has been written concerning Him in the songs of David, as it says, 'Elohim stands in the divine assembly, in the midst of Elohim He judges [Ps 82:1].' He said, 'Above it, to the heights, return. El will judge the nations [Ps 7:8-9].' When he said, 'How long will you judge unjustly and show impartiality to the wicked? Selah [Ps 82:2].' Its interpretation concerns Belial and the spirits of his lot who turn away from the commandments of El in wickedness. Melchizedek will exact the vengeances of the judgments of El...

"This is the 'Day of Peace' about which God spoke through Isaiah the prophet [52:7] who said, 'How beautiful on the mountains are the feet of the Messenger who proclaims peace, the Messenger of good who proclaims salvation, saying to Zion, "Your God reigns!"' Its interpretation is that the mountains are prophets' predictions about the Messenger and the Messenger is the one anointed of the Spirit about whom Daniel said, 'Until Messiah, the Prince, (there will be) seven weeks [Dan 9:25].' He is the Messenger of good who proclaims salvation. He is the one about whom it is written, when it says, 'to comfort those who mourn... [Isa 61:2-3],' to 'instruct them in all the ages of the world in truth.'

Ancient Testaments of the Patriarchs

"Zion is those who uphold the covenant, those who turn aside from walking in the ways of the people. But 'your God' is Melchizedek, who will save them from the hand of Belial. As for that which he has said, 'You will blow the signal-horn in the seventh month [Lev 23:24 or 25:9].' ...the divisions of the times..."

4Q385a fragment 5
"...three priests who will not walk in the ways of the former priests, who completely followed the God of Israel. In their days, pride will cause many to act wickedly against the covenant and become the slaves of foreign things. Israel will be rent asunder in that generation, each man fighting against his neighbor over the Torah and the Covenant. I will send hunger upon the land, but not for bread or water, but to hear the Word of the Lord."

4Q387
"...at the completion of ten jubilees, Israel will be walking in madness..."

4Q252 Col. 5
"'The scepter shall not depart from the tribe of Judah [Gen. 49:10].' The interpretation is while Israel has self-rule, there will not be anyone cut off who sits on the throne of David, for 'the staff' represents the covenant of kingship, and 'the standards' are the thousands of Israel. ...until the Messiah of righteousness comes, the branch of David [Isa. 11:1-2; Zech. 3:8], for to Him and His children have been given the covenant of the kingship of

His people for everlasting generations… it is the assembly of the men of…"

Florilegium

"Yahweh declares that He will build a house for David, and He shall set up his seed after him, and shall establish his royal throne forever. 'I shall be to him as a father, and he will be to Me as a son [2 Sam. 7:13-14].' He is 'the Shoot of David' who will arise with the Interpreter of the Law, who… in Zion in the last days; as it is written, 'And I shall raise up the tabernacle of David that is fallen [Amos 9:11; Acts 15:16].' That 'tabernacle of David that is fallen' is He who will arise to save Israel…

"'Why do the nations rage and the peoples imagine a vain thing? The kings of the earth set themselves, and the rulers take counsel together against the LORD and against His Messiah [Psalm 2:1-2].' The interpretation of the passage is that the nations and rulers will come against the Elect of Israel in the last days. This will be a 'time of trial' that is coming … as it is written in the book of Daniel the prophet, 'For the wicked to act wickedly [Dan. 11:32], the righteous shall make themselves white and purify themselves [Dan. 11:35],' and 'a people knowing God will seize [Dan. 11:32] …' The interpretation is after the… when he goes down from…"

Other Books by Ken Johnson, Th.D.

- **Ancient Post-Flood History,** Historical Documents That Point to a Biblical Creation.
- **Ancient Seder Olam,** A Christian Translation of the 2000-year-old Scroll
- **Ancient Prophecies Revealed,** 500 Prophecies Listed In Order Of When They Were Fulfilled
- **Ancient Book of Jasher,** Referenced in Joshua 10:13; 2 Samuel 1:18; 2 Timothy 3:8
- **Third Corinthians,** Ancient Gnostics and the End of the World
- **Ancient Paganism,** The Sorcery of the Fallen Angels
- **The Rapture,** The Pretribulational Rapture of the Church Viewed from the Bible and the Ancient Church
- **Ancient Epistle of Barnabas,** His Life and Teaching
- **The Ancient Church Fathers,** What the Disciples of the Apostles Taught
- **Ancient Book of Daniel**
- **Ancient Epistles of John and Jude**
- **Ancient Messianic Festivals,** And The Prophecies They Reveal
- **Ancient Word of God**
- **Cults and the Trinity**
- **Ancient Book of Enoch**
- **Ancient Epistles of Timothy and Titus**
- **Fallen Angels**

- **Ancient Book of Jubilees**
- **The Gnostic Origins of Calvinism**
- **The Gnostic Origins of Roman Catholicism**
- **Demonic Gospels**
- **The Pre-Flood Origins of Astrology**
- **The End-Times by the Church Fathers**
- **Ancient Book of Gad the Seer**
- **DVD 1 – The Prophetic Timeline**
- **DVD 2 – The Church Age**

For more information, visit us at:

Biblefacts.org

Bibliography

Schaff, Philip, *Ante-Nicene Fathers*, Eerdmans Publishing, 1893
Ken Johnson, *Ancient Book of Enoch*, Createspace, 2012
Ken Johnson, *Ancient Book of Jubilees*, Createspace, 2013
Ken Johnson, *Ancient Book of Gad the Seer*, Createspace, 2016
Ken Johnson, *Ancient Post-Flood History*, Createspace, 2010

Made in the USA
Columbia, SC
25 September 2018